ONE MAN

WESLEY
PENNINGTON

UrbanPress
INTERNACIONAL

One Man
by Wesley Pennington
Copyright ©2023 Wesley Pennington

ISBN 978-1-63360-232-8

For Worldwide Distribution
Printed in the USA

Urban Press
P.O. Box 8881
Pittsburgh, PA 15221-0881
412.646.2780
urbanpress.us

CONTENTS

Foreword   v

Preface   ix

Introduction   xi

Chapter 1
Let's Get Started   1

Chapter 2
The Role of Son   10

Chapter 3
The Role of Brother   19

Chapter 4
The Role of Friend   30

Chapter 5
The Role of Father   40

Chapter 6
The Role of Husband   48

Chapter 7
The Role of Mentor   57

Chapter 8
The Role of Leader   68

Chapter 9
All in One   78

Chapter 10
Some Good Role Models   89

Chatper 11
A Final Final Thought   97

Eight Virtues of Rally Point Ministries   111
More About the Author   113
Contact Info   115

FOREWORD

I invested enough time with superstars and serial killers, courageous heroes and vile killers, to uncover a common denominator within the narratives of the these men – a profoundly impactful relationship with Dad. In some cases, the bond was exceedingly beneficial. In other cases, the bond or lack of bond was unspeakably detrimental. Either way, the stories of good and bad guys accentuate the indisputable fact that the role of a father is pivotal in who we become. My name is Dr. Michael A.Caparrelli Jr. and I am a resigned pastor of 16 years, a present-day professor of psychology at three colleges, an author of four books, a researcher of human behavior, and perhaps most notably, the son of Michael A. Caparrelli Sr.

Have you noticed in the Bible that men are often introduced as the son of someone? Ancient wisdom emphasized sonship as a pivotal factor in a boy's passage into manhood. Hence, the reason the Bible introduces us to "Isaac, the son of Abraham, David, the son of a Jesse, Jesus, the son of God, etc." Many surnames – even in our modern Western culture – still carry the vestiges of this ancient wisdom. Names such as Johnson means "the son of John," Ben-Hur means "the son of Hur," and McDonald means "the son of Donald." Men were known in respect to their fathers because sonship was understood by the ancients as a basis for personal identity.

Who you are is shaped by whose you are. Dean Martin hit it on the head with the timeless lyric, "You're nobody until somebody loves you." No surprise that the stats show 71% of high school dropouts, 90% of all runaway kids, and 60% of all youth suicides are fatherless kids.[1] Some fatherless kids are dad-deficient, which means they grew up without the physical presence of a dad. In these cases, the bond with dad is a hypothetical reality that cloaks them with an orphan mentality. An orphan mentality consists of sensitivity to rejection, uneasiness with criticism, emotionally shallow, and angry with the world. Others are dad-distant, which means they grew up without the emotional availability of a dad. In these cases, the bond with Dad allowed them no opportunity to know or be known, love or be loved. Either case, dad-deficient or dad-distant, a boy is left feeling like he's nobody when he belongs to nobody.

Between 2022-2023, I conducted a 100-hour case study at Shawangunk Correctional Facility on a convicted infamous serial killer by the name of David Berkowitz. Thankfully, David is a born- again believer today who shares his testimony with other inmates, discipling 15 guys within the prison, as well as corresponding with people from around the world through snail-mail. David unashamedly testifies to everyone about his transformation resultant from a daily, vibrant relationship with his Heavenly Father. Yet, back in the 1970s, he shot

[1]Jack Brewer. *Fatherlessness and its Effects on American Society.* (AFPI, February 15, 2022).

15 innocent people with a .44 Caliber on the streets of New York City. I wasn't shocked to discover that a dad-distant relationship played a critical role in the making of the massacre. While Nat Berkowitz was a man of integrity, he worked long days at his hardware store in the Bronx, leaving David feeling emotionally deprived. The moniker that David chose to describe himself in a letter addressed to the NYPD during his killing spree said everything about his yearning for a father – "the son of Sam."

The beauty of *One Man* is that it colorfully and profoundly describes what it means to be a son in a culture where the definition of masculinity is diluted. *One Man* is no puddle-deep manuscript written without deep analysis, but instead gleans it's truths from the Bible, modern psychology, historical anecdotes, and the author's own radical journey. But it doesn't stop with sonship! The author also elucidates on how sonship intersects with a variety of the roles that a man plays as a brother, friend, father, mentor and leader. Lastly, the reader is afforded the opportunity to introspect at the end of every chapter with a series of self-reflective questions that will help him examine and challenge himself in every important area of life. This book is not written for chumps but champs who are courageous enough to gaze in the mirror of God's word and discover who they were designed to be.

On a personal note, I have known author Wesley Pennington for nearly two decades on a deep level. He worked alongside me between 2008-2019 while planting a church in Rhode Island that reached out to troubled men – the angry, addicted, and alienated. Through that time, I witnessed Wes' own metamorphosis from a stoic war hero and an emotionally-guarded police officer into a loving, transparent man of God. I watched firsthand how Wes led countless men into freedom from their own childhood ghosts through up-close and personal mentorship. What's most significant to note is that Wes' transformation was only possible because of his willingness to be fathered by seasoned men within our congregation as well as being loved by the Father in Heaven. Wes learned how to be loved, or also stated, to be the beloved. I couldn't think of a better son of God to author this particular manuscript.

The poet, Anne Sexton, once wrote, "It's not who my father was that matters. It's who I remember he was." Her poignant verse highlights the fact that father impressions, etched into our souls at a young age, shape who we become in every domain of life. By the time I was 18 years old, I was hospitalized two times for suicide attempts and incarcerated in a juvenile detention center for auto theft and home invasions. During that era, I suffered with an orphan mentality from years of dad distance whereby I visited my father in prison and lived an emotionally estranged existence from him when he was home. Decades later, I am privileged with a life of deep fulfillment, parenting children and stepchildren, married to my soulmate and making a positive difference in the world. Why? Because my name is Michael A. Caparrelli Jr., and I am a son of God who has learned and is learning how to be *One Man*.

Michael A. Caparrelli Jr.
PhD Behavioral Science
Minister of the Gospel of Jesus Christ

PREFACE

Special Note on Being One Man

"Be the same person privately, publicly, and personally." – Judah Smith

I have a prayer that I say every day, which is, "Lord, make into the one man that you have called me to be." When I pray this, I am proclaiming that I want to be the same man in *every* aspect of my life. No matter where I am or what I am doing, I want to be the one man of God in it all. I do not wish to be a father without God, or a husband without God, or even a boss or employee without God being right there with me.

If you have read any of my previous books, *Through the Smoker: How God Operates in a Man's Life*, or *The Love of the Father: Abba's Plan to Restore the Family*, you would have read about my work as a Rhode Island state trooper and how hard it was for me to be the one man of God in this area of my life. I had to dispense justice but with the heart of God; to deal with the pains of the community while at the same time operating with and motivated by the love of God. Let me tell you it was not easy to do.

There were many times when I started to become the trooper who hated people because we mostly saw their bad side. But my prayer would always remind me that the Lord wants me to be the one man of God in every part of my life – even as a trooper for the Rhode Island state police. I came to realize in time that Jesus can operate in every part of my life, even as a law enforcement officer. However, that required me to continually allow the Lord to live in and through me. At times, I had to repent and start over because of my sinful ways. But through it all, I hope that those with whom I worked saw me as the one man of God that I was in every other role that I play in my life.

My passion is to see all of us function as the one man of God in all the roles we play. I pray as you read this book you will be challenged to look at your life and address those places where you might not have allowed Jesus to enter – yet. Then I hope I inspire and equip you to take that all-important step to invite Him in to that particular area.

By doing so, you will become the one man of God that you are called to be.

INTRODUCTION

I am Pastor Wesley Pennington, and I am the president of an organization called Rally Point Men's Ministries. You can look at my bio at the end of this book to see the things I have done in my life, which I think qualify me to speak on men's topics. I have been called to speak to the hearts of men by our Lord and Savior Jesus Christ. This is the third book I have written in an attempt to equip men for their high calling in Christ.

One of the gifts the Lord has given me is the ability to see the inner workings of a man's life. My first book, *Through the Smoker*, describes how God transforms a man. In it, I use the analogy of a smoked brisket to portray this process. My love of BBQ and my love for the Lord are brought together in this book. I also include a brisket recipe that alone is worth the purchase price!

My second book is called *The Love of the Father: Abba's Plan to Restore the Family*. In this book, I compare fatherhood to Abba Father and His example of fatherhood. I look at the problems of modern fatherhood and then include some possible solutions. I conclude that we don't have to worry because Abba has a plan and that plan is in full effect.

In this my third book, *One Man*, I will look at the roles men can have in our everyday lives. We will take each role and look at it in more depth through the lens of Jesus. As you read this book, I hope it encourages you to want to better fulfill each role you play in your life. I also pray that you will look for new ways to include God in each role. At the end of each chapter, I give you a final thought by providing a case study of someone or a situation in the Bible that personifies the role we discussed.

I also provide some reflection questions that you can use to further ponder the role we discussed, or to use in a small group setting. You will also find some additional references to look up and study on your own time. I hope that this book becomes a study guide for you as you look to enhance the roles you have in your life.

As the leader of the Rally Point Men's Ministry, I host a weekly meeting when we discuss how to be a better man of God, often focusing for several weeks on a specific topic. One of the topics we discussed recently was the roles of a man of God. The conversations and discussion indicated to me that we as men don't understand the various roles we play.

Furthermore, we don't understand how we should or can flow from role to role. It is human nature to conform to our culture and become the person we are expected to be. That means if I am being father then I naturally flow into the father role without even thinking about it. This is good and bad for several reasons. Let me explain it like this.

When you encountered Jesus, you found salvation and forgiveness for your sins. Perhaps you got radically saved by our Lord and Savior who delivered you from a futile and sinful lifestyle. The challenge after that is that we play so many roles that we slide from one role to the next without thinking much about it and sometimes we forget to bring Jesus with us. So, it's not uncommon for us to have a men's meeting filled with the Holy Spirit, only to hear men using profanity as we eat breakfast together. Their posture and demeanor totally changed from one role, a man in a church meeting, to the next where they were a man among a group of men who were socializing.

As a Rhode Island state trooper, I become the trooper when I put my uniform on. But at the end of the day when I got home and took the uniform off, I no longer acted like a trooper. I was so used to sliding from being a trooper to being a civilian that I never noticed it. As a civilian I would pray and read the Word, but as a trooper I had no time for that. Consequently, I had God in one part of my life but not in another part. When we had group conversations as a trooper, I realized I wasn't bring Jesus with me from one role to the next. And I was struggling to understand why I was blessed in one area of my life but not in the other.

The roles I mention in this book are just a few of the main roles we all play. I'm sure there are more, but I trust you will be able to take the concept and the practices I share and apply them to whatever role God has you in at any given time.

Thank you for picking this book up and I hope that by the time you finish, your prayer will be "Lord, make me into the *one* man of God I'm called to be."

Wesley Pennington
Coventry, Rhode Island
November 2023

Chapter 1

LET'S GET STARTED

"He humbled you, causing you to hunger and then feeding you with manna, which neither you nor your ancestors had known, to teach you that man does not live by bread alone but on every word that comes from the mouth of the Lord."
– Deuteronomy 8:3

"Man is the only creature who refuses to be what he is." – Albert Camus

I struggle to know how or where to even start this book. With a title like *One Man*, there can be so many places to start and then go. What drives me to write this book, however, is a study I recently completed with our men's group at Sacred Exchange Fellowship, during which we completed a five-week study on relationships. During those sessions, the

Holy Spirit compelled me to speak to the men about the various relationships we have.

I have learned that in a man's life, it's the relationships he has that will either make or break him. Also, the decisions we must make in those relationships cause us to walk taller and more confidently, or to stumble and fall. So, after we finished the five-week study (it was only supposed to be one Bible study), I felt it was a confirmation for me to write this book.

As I examine my life, I see there are many roles that I play. The problem is that so many of us wear a different mask in each role. Let me explain. If I am the father, I put on my father mask. If I am the friend, I put on the friend mask and so on. One of my prayers I pray every day is "Lord, make me the one man of God You have called me to be." That indicates my desire to be the same man in all my roles, meaning being the man of God I was called to be.

I think of this as integrity, being the same man and having the same set of behavioral values at home, at church, at work, and in any other role God gives me. In fact, integrity can also be understood as wholeness or consistency. People don't have to wonder what version of Wes is going to show up; I'm the same no matter where I am or what I'm doing.

I understand that we have different roles to play in our lives as men, but that doesn't mean we need to change who we are. That's why I have titled this book *One Man* because my desire is to encourage you to be the one man of God that you are called to be in all the roles you hold.

In this book, I will go through each role, and we will see what Scripture says about how and what we should be. We will discuss the role of son, brother, friend, father, husband, mentor, and leader. Through these roles, God uses us to affect others.

I often lecture police officers and community members on implicit bias. In this training, we discuss the things we carry in us that can and often do persuade us to make decisions. When we are men of God, all our discussions should be led by the Holy Spirit. We would love for that to be completely true and possible for us in every instance, but we sometimes make decisions that cause us to be Spirit-led in one instance but not in the next.

There's a YouTube video I showed in the class that's a story about a teacher who changed a little boy's world just by allowing the boy to be what he was called to be. The little boy would sit in his seat and fiddle with his hands during class. It got to the point where other teachers would send the little boy to the principal's office. One day he was fiddling with his hands in this teacher's class and was made to stay after school. The little boy thought to himself, *I am in trouble.*

The teacher then said, "You're not in trouble. In fact, I don't think you have a problem at all, I think you're a drummer." The teacher then goes into his drawer and pulls out the boy's first pair of drumsticks. The little boy goes on to become one of the world's best drummers, all because of that one moment in time when someone saw him for who he was, not who they interpreted him to be. I love when the little boy (who is actually the man telling the story in the video) says, "It's not the point to be the best in the world, but to be the best for the world."

The Lord wants us to be who we are that is the best for the world. The only way we can be the best for the world is to live by every word that comes from the mouth of the Lord. I am not writing this to be legalistic or unrealistic in any way. If you have read any of my books, you know I like to be as transparent as I can be about myself and the material I am sharing.

Let me say this as we start: I haven't always lived by every word that comes from the mouth of the Lord. In fact, at one point in time I was the worst of the sinners in not doing what I thought was right and good. Proverbs 14:12 says, "There is a way that appears to be right, but in the end, it leads to death," and I was heading to death. Even when I found the Lord and started to walk with him, I was still doing what appeared right to me. Are you also doing what appears right to you? Ask yourself as you read this, "Am I being honest with myself?" That's where we need to start if we want to be the man God has called us to be.

My brother, I tried to do what appeared right to me and all it did was bring me disaster – one failed relationship after another, failing in the workplace time and time again. Is this resonating with you? Isaiah 55:8 states, "'For my thoughts are not your thoughts, neither are your ways my ways,' declares the Lord." As men, we are called out from a world that does not know God, so often our ways are so far from His ways that we could never get to Him without help.

As a man of God, you ways should line up with His ways and that happens once you meet Jesus and accept Him as your Savior. Then the process of becoming like Him takes place. If you want to read more on that, get my book *Through the Smoker* to further understand how God prepares and transforms people.

Because we are raised in a world that does not know God and then we meet God and start to grow in Him, we don't sense there is anything wrong with our thinking. However, our thought process must improve and align itself with every word that comes from the mouth of God as expressed in His Word, the Bible. That explains why we make so many mis-steps at first – and even later in our walk – because we continue to take matters into our own hands. Once we do things as we think they should be done, disaster is right around the corner.

As you read, I hope to answer your questions that are similar to the ones I have been asked in our men's group at Sacred Exchange Fellowship. These are questions like: *How should we treat the people in our various relationships? How does Jesus want us to treat each other?* And my favorite question is: *Why is it important to have open and honest relationships?* There are so many more questions that we have discussed over the years, and I will touch on them, and others, as we go on.

At the end of life, it doesn't matter how much stuff we have acquired. It will not be about how much money we were able to make. It will be about relationships and how we managed them. Did we allow the call of God in our lives to infect others? It's even going to be about relationships when we all get to heaven as Jesus indicated in Mark 12:28-34:

> One of the teachers of the law came and heard them debating. Noticing that Jesus had given them a good answer, he asked him, "Of all the commandments, which is the most important?"
>
> "The most important one," answered Jesus, "is this: 'Hear, O Israel: The Lord our God, the Lord is one. Love the Lord your God with all your heart and with all your soul and with all your mind and with all your strength.' The second is this: 'Love your neighbor as yourself.' There is no commandment greater than these."
>
> "Well said, teacher," the man replied. "You are right in saying that God is one and there is no other but him. To love him with all your heart, with all your understanding and with all your strength, and to love your neighbor as yourself is more important than all burnt offerings and sacrifices."
>
> When Jesus saw that he had answered wisely, he said to him, "You are not far from the kingdom of God." And from then on no one dared ask him any more questions.

We will discuss relationships in depth in

this book. Man of God, you were called to be relational. Our God is relational, which is why He created us so He can have many sons and daughters.

We get caught up with being set apart from the world, and we are, but not so that we become loners, never affecting the world as we should. We are called to affect the world, to be world changers, for, after all, we are sons of Abba. We can't affect and change the world if we go through our relationships as if they don't mean anything to us.

Remember it's not important to be the best in the world, but to be the best for the world. Our Lord Jesus Christ is the best for the world and calls us to be also. The way we can be the best for the world is through the relationships we foster. The most important ones are between us and Abba, between us and Jesus, and between us and the Holy Spirit.

In the Bible, we read again and again of mighty men helping, saving, and encouraging others. After all, the mission of Jesus was to save us all. That happened through His relationship with the Father. Plainly put, Abba Father made us to be relational. Every call from God involves serving, loving, or impacting others in some way, shape, or form. Doesn't it then make sense that it matters how we treat others?

We have been given a command to love others as we love ourselves. Let that sink in for a minute. What does that mean to and for you? Let's look at that and go through it together in this book.

Man of God, you are called to be relational!

FINAL THOUGHT

Jesus stated that there are two great commandments when asked what the greatest commandment is. He said to love God and then also to love your neighbor as you love yourself. If we took the time to look at the commandments, we would see that they are all about relationships. The problem we have had is that there are parts of us that we do not love. Maybe we do not love them because we have not invited Jesus into them. In order for us to love our neighbors as we love ourselves, we must have Jesus present and working in all the roles we play.

We are going to discuss each role and then at the end of each chapter, we will look at someone who exemplifies that role in the Bible. Let's get started.

REFLECTION QUESTIONS

1. Do we need other people in our lives? If so, why?
2. How are your relationships? Are they good or are you having trouble getting along?
3. Do you blame others when your relationships go bad?
4. As a man of God, what is your responsibility in your relationships?

ADDITIONAL REFERENCES

Acts 13:48
Romans 12:18
Ephesians 1:4-5
Colossians 3:5
1 Peter 4:8

Chapter 2

THE ROLE
OF SON

*"He is the radiance of the glory of God
and the exact imprint of His nature. And
He upholds the universe by the word of
His power. After making purification for
sins, He sat down at the right hand of the
Majesty on high."* – Hebrews 1:3

To love your neighbor as yourself is a difficult task. In order to do this, you must understand the role you play as a son of God, which involves becoming like the father. Colossians 1:15-20 explains,

> The Son is the image of the invisible God, the firstborn over all creation. For in him all things were created: things in heaven and on earth, visible and invisible, whether thrones or powers or rulers or authorities; all things have been created through him and

for him. He is before all things, and in him all things hold together. And he is the head of the body, the church; he is the beginning and the firstborn from among the dead, so that in everything he might have the supremacy. For God was pleased to have all his fullness dwell in him, and through him to reconcile to himself all things, whether things on earth or things in heaven, by making peace through his blood, shed on the cross.

This is quite a passage, but let me give you a quick overview of what I see in it. It all started with Jesus as the first Son of Abba. He knew His role as a Son. Jesus Himself said, "Anyone who has seen me has seen the Father" (John 14:9), meaning that Jesus was the exact replica of Abba our Father. Then Paul wrote in Romans 2:29, "For those God foreknew he also predestined to be conformed to the image of his Son, that he might be the firstborn among many brothers and sisters." Now we are to be like Him in every way through the transformative power of the Spirit. Man of God, our first role is the role of son.

I'm delighted I get to tell you that you are a son of Abba. I love telling men everywhere that they are sons of Abba. Identity is key to success in our walk as Christians. If we know who we are, then we know who we belong to, and the anointing of God starts to flow in our lives. That's another book to write for another day. But truth is, the moment you become a Christian and are saved by grace through accepting Jesus as your Savior, you become a son of God.

What is the role of a son in the Kingdom of God? This is simple in its presentation but extremely difficult in its execution. The role of the son in Abba's Kingdom is to become more like Him – to become like the Father just like Jesus is as we read in Romans 8:29. Have you ever had someone say you look just like your father? This is the goal of the Spirit who is now working within you. As we speak, the Spirit of God along with Jesus Himself are working to transform you into the image of Jesus and thus, the image of the Father.

Remember that sonship is the process of becoming like the father. In 1 John 4:14-15, John wrote, "And we have seen and testify that the Father has sent his Son to be the Savior of the world. If anyone acknowledges that Jesus is the Son of God, God lives in them and they in God." When you become like the Father, you are a true son of God in every sense of the word. And that not only means you look like the Father, you also act like Him. You feel what He feels and thus act out of love for others just as He does.

The problem we have is that often we do not know how to be sons. The reason is because most of us have had to grow up without the father figure in the house – or we did not have a good father figure in the house. It is hard for the son to understand the love of the father if the father is never there. I am one of the blessed ones, I suppose. My father was in the house and worked hard to put clothes on my back and food in my stomach. You may say that was a good thing, which of course it was. However, what was missing was more important than clothes and food. The thing that was missing was never having heard, "This is my son who I am proud of."

A father's affirmation of his son is important. If we pay attention, we see that Abba affirmed Jesus as His Son on several occasions:

> And a voice from heaven said, "This is my Son, whom I love; with him I am well pleased" (Matthew 3:17).

> While he was still speaking, a bright cloud covered them, and a voice from the cloud said, "This is my Son, whom I love; with him I am well pleased. Listen to him!" (Matthew 17:5).

This must have been quite an encouragement for Jesus. It reassured Him of the mission and authority He had from the Father. There are no greater words of affirmation for any son to hear than the words, "This is my son." I can't remember my father ever saying, "I love you, Son." He showed he did by his actions and I know his generation wasn't in the habit of saying that, for no one had ever said it to them.

But I missed the affirmation from my father that would have established me as a man in his eyes. I wrote a book to fathers titled *The Love of the Father*, which goes into detail on the problem of fathers, but I digress for we're talking about the role of the son. I just wanted to point out how sometimes we're unable to be sons because of a lack of fathers.

If you're reading this and you're not feeling much like a son of God, let me say this: *You are a son of God*. Ephesians 1:4-6 states,

> For he chose us in him before the creation of the world to be holy and blameless in his sight. In love he predestined us for adoption to sonship through Jesus Christ, in accordance with his pleasure and will—to the praise of his glorious grace, which he has freely given us in the One he loves.

As you read that, you should be running around your house shouting, "Thank You, Lord!" Did you notice the term *sonship* in that passage? It said, "adoption to sonship through Jesus Christ." Sonship is the process of becoming like the father. Abba accomplishes this through Jesus Christ and this adoption is not like what we know to be adoption. This is more like the story of Pinocchio when a wooden marionette became real live flesh and blood. That was a radical transformation and so is ours. We're made new creatures, actually a new species, in Christ!

This adoption makes us full-blooded begotten children of Abba through Jesus Christ. So, when I say you're a son of God, it represents a divine act. This is the most important role that we play as men of God. This is the reason I am starting this book with the topic of sonship because that's where it all starts.

Galatians 4:6-7 says,

> Because you are his sons, God sent the Spirit of his Son into our hearts, the

Spirit who calls out, "Abba, Father."
So you are no longer a slave, but God's
child; and since you are his child, God
has made you also an heir.

If you've never been encouraged before
in your relationship with God and walk with
Christ, be encouraged now. Every son is enti-
tled to an inheritance from his father and you
have one as a son of God. Not only are you a
son, but you are also an heir to the kingdom
of Heaven. We have to establish this while we
are still here on earth before we go to heaven
to be with Abba.

Man of God, your most important role is
as a son because as a son it is your duty to allow yourself to be in relationship with Abba.
It is all about relationship because when we
know we are loved by Abba, then we in turn
love Abba. This enables us to enter into a deep
relationship with Jesus and Abba, solidifying
our position in our heavenly family while still
here on earth. This then gives us what we need
to relate properly to the rest of God's family
here on earth.

You may struggle with this truth because of the lack of affirmation from your
father. But Jesus has a remedy for that and it
starts by Jesus bringing us through the smoker and transforming us into the true sons we
are called to be. On our way through, we get
to know what it feels like to be a beloved son.
Our only job in the process is to allow Jesus to
bring us through, allowing Abba to transform
us into His likeness.

Listen to me, my brother. Before you can

be anything else or be in any other relationship or play any other role, you first have to come to the place of being a son. Everything else flows from that knowledge. You can't be a good father if you've never become a son. You can't be a good husband if you've never become a son. You can't become a good brother if you haven't first become a son.

I could go on and on about the role of the son but let's go on to the role of the brother in the next chapter, where I have much to say about the importance of brotherhood.

FINAL THOUGHT

I could make this easy and talk about the Son of God, but He comes later. Let's discuss the son of David and Bathsheba by the name of Solomon. Solomon became king of Israel after a revolt by his brother who threatened to take his role, but David came through and made Solomon king of Israel. Solomon was a good son listening to his father and learning from him. We know he was a good son because the first thing he did as king was sacrifice to God. He had a love for God just like David his father.

I love the part of the story when God asked Solomon to request anything he wanted and God would give it to him. Solomon could have asked for riches or fame; he could have asked for the death of his foes; he could have asked for women and long life. But he did not ask for any of those things; instead he asked for wisdom.

It took wisdom for Solomon to know that he needed wisdom. He had watched his father and knew that the people he would rule were a stubborn group. Solomon exemplified the role of son. He even built the temple that David his father wanted to build. Take some time and look at the life of Solomon. I know in the end he falls off the path but he was still a beloved son of David and of God.

REFLECTION QUESTIONS

1. Do you feel like a son?
2. How was your relationship with your father?
3. Can you see now that you a son of God?
4. Are you encouraged to know that Abba has made you an heir?

ADDITIONAL REFERENCES

Matthew 28:19
John 1:3
John 3:16
John 20:31
Hebrews 1:3

Chapter 3

THE ROLE OF BROTHER

"The beauty of genuine brotherhood and peace is more precious than diamonds or silver or gold." – Dr. Martin Luther King Jr.

"Whoever does God's will is my brother and sister and mother." – Mark 3:35

This is the perfect verse to start this chapter. Jesus is saying that whoever does the will of His Abba is His (Jesus') brother. What does it mean to be a brother? If we are all becoming like the father and made into sons, then that means we are all brothers. We are brothers in Christ and one day to be begotten brothers of God, brothers of the same kind and blood. How beautiful is it for brothers to get along?

There are many Scriptures that talk about the love of one brother for another. Proverbs 17:17 says, "A friend loves as all times and a brother is born for times of adversity." This is why when men go off to war and encounter various kinds of hardship, they become brothers – bonded together by a common experience and purpose.

In fact, one of my favorite television shows of all time is titled *A Band of Brothers*. I could watch that series again and again because it depicts how men who go through something incredibly hard together form a bond and alliance deeper than friendship. It forms brothers. One of the roles that we play as a man of God is to be a brother.

You may never have had a biological brother in your life, but that does not disqualify you from being a brother. That's because our Father in heaven calls us to be brothers. It is not biological; it is a call, a mandate from God Himself. He then goes about the process of equipping us to be brothers. When we accept Jesus as our Lord and Savior, the Spirit of God comes and starts to transform us into the image of Jesus. Therefore, becoming like Jesus is becoming a brother in Christ:

> For those who are led by the Spirit of God are the children of God. The Spirit you received does not make you slaves, so that you live in fear again; rather, the Spirit you received brought about your adoption to sonship. And by him we cry, "*Abba*, Father." The Spirit himself testifies with our spirit that we are God's children. Now if we are children, then we are heirs—heirs of God and co-heirs with Christ, if indeed we share in

his sufferings in order that we may also share in his glory (Romans 8:14-17).

If we're all children of God through Christ, then we're brothers and sisters because we have the same Father. In a sense, brotherhood is something we are called to but then we must learn what our duties and responsibilities are in that relationship.

I had a friend one time whose children were arguing and one of the children said, "You're not my sister anymore!" While that was easy to say, it was impossible to do – or undo. When you're born into God's family, you can't undo your brotherhood because you share the same Father with all the other children. You may choose to ignore, mistreat, or be bitter towards your brothers, but they're still your brothers – and you're theirs.

Marvin Gay wrote and sang a song for the ages titled *What's Goin' On?* And it's relevant for us, for we have to ask each other what's going on today. We live in a me-first world in which we have lost the concept of brotherly love. Proverbs 27:17 says, "As iron sharpens iron so does one person sharpen another." Brothers are made by going through things together, sharing common values and purpose. Those who I call a brother in my life are those with whom I have gone through some things.

But what's so amazing about the God we serve is that we don't have to go through things for us to be brothers. The Spirit unites us in a common cause when we become brothers in Christ. We may never have met before but because the Spirit joins us in a common cause we become brothers. You may ask what is the common cause that the Spirit brings us through? That would be the transformation that occurs from the inside out, making us into the image of Jesus Christ. Remember I said we become begotten sons of God.

This is a good place to explain what begotten means. *Begotten* is an Old English word and means *of the same kind*. An example would be dog, cats, man, and God. A dog begets a dog. A cat begets a cat, and humans another human being.

God is different than we are; He is of a different kind, made of different material and DNA. Jesus is of the same kind as God. We will be of the same kind as God when Jesus returns. The begotten part of who we are in Christ joins us together as brothers. So thank you, my brother, for accepting Jesus as your Lord and Savior and accepting your inheritance – a place in the body of Christ.

In 2023, our Rally Point Men of Integrity conference theme was "Who are You?" More than 200 men attended and the idea was to help them see who they are in Christ, that their identity is in the Lord – and they are true sons of God. Not only are they true sons of God but they are brothers with each other. It was powerful to see a man come to a conference and leave knowing that he had 199 other brothers. And that number was only how many were in the building at the time. The brotherhood of Jesus Christ spans the country and around the world.

I love what James wrote in James 4:11:

Brothers and sisters, do not slander one another. Anyone who speaks against a brother or sister or judges them speaks against the law and judges it. When you judge the law, you are not keeping it, but in judgment on it.

This says it all for me. The world tells you to judge your brother but the Lord says *not* to judge him. Jesus said in Matthew 7:2 that "in the same way you judge you will be judged." So be careful, my brother, because we should treat each other with brotherly love and acceptance. Jesus said the greatest commandment is love the Lord your God with all your mind and heart and strength, and the second is like it and that's to love your neighbor as yourself. The more I study and think about what Jesus said, I realize it's all about loving our brothers and sisters.

In God's eyes, we're all brothers and sisters until the clock stops. Once the clock stops, those who have not accepted Jesus as their Savior will have to stand before God and answer why they refused His invitation. Man of God, if we call ourselves sons and if we call ourselves men of God, then we must be able to walk also in brotherly love.

I once asked Abba Father a question about who the sons of God are that are mentioned in Genesis 6 and the story of Noah. I do not know about you but when I ask the Lord a question like that, He usually sends me on an intensive search. True to form, I went on my search and I found there are two thoughts on who the sons of God were who are mentioned in Genesis. Some believe they were fallen angels and others believe that they were the offspring of Seth who had sex with the daughters of Cain.

Either way you look at it, God brought me back to Noah and revealed that those who are obedient to Him are the sons of God. I wish Abba had just brought me to Mark 3 and that would have answered it. Jesus gave the same answer that I had learned through my hours of research:

> Then Jesus' mother and brothers arrived. Standing outside, they sent someone in to call him. A crowd was sitting around him, and they told him, "Your mother and brothers are outside looking for you." "Who are my mother and my brothers?" he asked. Then he looked at those seated in a circle around him and said, "Here are my mother and my brothers! Whoever does God's will is my brother and sister and mother" (Mark 3:31-35).

We become brothers through the power of the Spirit's transformation as we are obedient. That makes me want to run around the room every time I think of it. The Spirit given to us leads us and also transforms us into the image of Jesus. We become brothers of the bravest, most courageous, loving brother of all time, Jesus Christ. We all go through the process and at the end of it, we all will see each other in heaven and call each other brother. This is why one of the roles we have as a man of God is the role of brother. We must learn down here how to be brothers before we get up there – before we get to heaven!

Like I said earlier, you may not have had a biological brother but God has given you many brothers as one of the roles you now have to assume. Each role we have is vital because it teaches us something about Abba and about ourselves – the relationship between God and man and between man and man. It is like a triangle where God sits at the point of the triangle, and we are at the corners and the relationship goes up the triangle and side to side along the triangle. This is a reality because of the shed blood of Jesus which covers us, redeems us, and adopts us.

A brother should always lift up and encourage another brother. Sadly, I often see men of God putting down other men of God, speaking against them or gossiping about them. This is not what our Father in heaven had in mind for us. One man sharpens another brother and lifts up his spirits. Jesus lifted up each one of us by dying on the cross. He elevated us in the sight of Abba our Father in heaven and we should follow in His footsteps.

I recently went to an art exhibit featuring the work of Vincent Van Gogh and had a chance to read the correspondence between Vincent and Theo, his brother. It was through Theo Van Gogh that Vincent's work had a voice. Theo's love for, dedication to, and faith in his brother's immense talent ensured Vincent's legacy. Bound by more than brotherhood, Vincent and Theo unknowingly shared a body of words and love that transcend time and still resonate today. That's what brothers are supposed to do for each other. This is the role of a man of God: to lift up his brother and help him when needed.

I'm reminded of the parable of the good Samaritan in Luke 10:25-37. After the rabbi and the priest walked by and refused to help the man who was injured on the side of the road, a man came by who was a Samaritan and helped the man. After bringing him to the inn, the good Samaritan gave the innkeeper some money and told him to take care of the man and if it was more than what he gave him, the Samaritan would take care of it on his next visit.

Now of course I paraphrased this story but suffice it to say that this is what brotherhood looks like: one man lifting up another, supporting another and encouraging another man. I believe this is what Abba and Jesus envision for every man of God. The role of brotherhood for the man of God is vital for his walk with God.

I believe at the end of this walk on earth, we will be judged according to the quality of our relationships. It will not matter the amount of stuff we have or the money we gave away. What will matter is our relationships with Jesus and our relationship with one another. The standard will be, man of God, whether or not you were a good brother.

Man of God, you are a brother to many, which means you are not alone in this walk or your struggles. Jesus promised that anyone who is obedient to His Father is His brother.

That means He will be there for you and with you in your time of need. What's more, it's not just Jesus but every other man of God because they are called your brothers. Treat your relationships as precious jewels which will be displayed on the last day.

Proverbs 17:17 is worth mentioning again: "A friend loves at all times, and a brother is born for a time of adversity." Have you made yourself available for your brothers? Are you willing to go through some stuff with another man? This is what it means to be a brother. The role of a brother is one that will strengthen you and build you up as you build up others. Bless you, man of God, and may He help you stand strong for your brother!

FINAL THOUGHT

Let's look at what a great brotherly relationship looks like and examine the relationship between David and Jonathan. This may seem like a strange example to you because they were not blood brothers, but they are brothers in ever sense of the word. They loved each other and would do anything for one another. Jonathan was supposed to be king because he was the son of Saul. But Jonathan didn't let that interfere with his relationship with David even though it was David who was going to be king instead of Jonathan.

David loved Jonathan so much that after Jonathan died and David became king, David graciously seated Jonathan's son Mephibosheth at his own royal table, treating Jonathan's son as his own. That is brotherhood at its finest. If we can come close to that example of brotherhood, we will make Abba proud.

REFLECTION QUESTIONS

1. When you look around, do you have other men in your life you can call brother?

2. Have you been vulnerable enough with other men to allow them into your life?

3. As a man of God, are you trustworthy enough to be looked at as a brother?

ADDITIONAL REFERENCES

Leviticus 19:34
Psalm 133:1
Proverbs 10:12
Matthew 5:41-42
Matthew 25:35-39

Chapter 4

THE ROLE OF FRIEND

"Do not be misled: 'Bad company corrupts good character.'" – 1 Corinthians 15:33

"Lots of people want to ride with you in the limo, but what you want is someone who will take the bus with you when the limo breaks down." – Oprah Winfrey

"Love is the only force capable of transforming an enemy into a friend." – Dr. Martin Luther King Jr.

I know it looks strange introducing this chapter with a verse stating that bad company corrupts good character. However, we have all seen the influence that our friends and associates can have on us for good or bad. It's often referred to as peer pressure. I always wondered why God instructed the Israelites not to have relationships with the people in the land after they went into the Promised Land. It's because what God was building and doing among the Israelites would be ruined if and when they encountered bad company.

Have you ever heard the saying "hang around a barnyard and you smell like the barnyard"? God understood this and did not want the Israelites to hang around with bad company or it would undo and hinder their holiness. The same is true today for you and me. If you are serious about being a man of God, you need to choose your friendships wisely.

You may be thinking that Jesus hung out the tax collectors and others who were considered undesirable. Yes, Jesus interacted with many so-called 'sinners,' but when you come right down to it, Jesus was close to only three men: His inner circle of James, John, and Peter. They were the ones who went up on the mountain of transfiguration with Him and took part in many other private sessions with Him.

As a man of God, you also need to have an inner circle, those men who are close to you and share everything with you. These are the men you can call in your dark hours in the middle of the night when you need help or advice. This kind of relationship can best be summarized by one word: friendship.

One of the best examples of friendships in the Bible is the one between David and Jonathan, who I highlighted at the end of the last chapter. In 1 Samuel 18:1-4, we read

> After David had finished talking with
> Saul, Jonathan became one in spirit

with David, and he loved him as himself. From that day Saul kept David with him and did not let him return home to his family. And Jonathan made a covenant with David because he loved him as himself. Jonathan took off the robe he was wearing and gave it to David, along with his tunic, and even his sword, his bow and his belt.

Jonathan saw in David a reflection of who he himself was, and this recognition pulled him outside himself and bound him to David. Here in this passage, we see that Jonathan and David had a committed friendship. David was not afraid to share everything with Jonathan and it was the same with Jonathan. In every man of God's life, he will need some friends and he will need to be that kind of friend for others. One of the things we were told since we were children was "you must learn to stand on your own two feet" or "do it alone; you don't need anyone else." This was bad advice, if not downright untruths, because God has put us here for each other.

A good friend will challenge us, causing us to grow. We therefore should take this role seriously. We will have a chance to watch someone's back as they in turn will look after ours. Jonathan had David's back when Saul wanted to kill him and warned David when Saul his father had murderous intentions against him. This is what friends do and what friends look like. In the friendship between Jonathan and David, God has shown us what friendship looks like.

There's a difference between men who are friends but not saved, and men who are saved and are friends. Let me give you an example. When I was young, I had a friend with whom I was quite close. We went everywhere together and many times ate and slept in each other's homes. We were inseparable. Neither one of us was following Jesus so in reality we had no idea what it meant to be friends. One day, we found ourselves arguing and bickering over young girls who we both liked. We found ourselves competing over everything and soon we were no longer friends.

As a saved man of God, I approach friendship differently than I did with my childhood friend. I have friends who I would trust with my life. We look to build each other up instead of knocking each other down. That's how our friendships as men of God should be. They should not only be for what we can get but for what we can give. They should look different than those who do not know Jesus. First Thessalonians 5:11 says, "Therefore encourage one another and build each other up, just as in fact you are doing." This is what a Christian friendship looks like.

Then there's another verse about friendship in Job 6:14: "Anyone who withholds kindness from a friend forsakes the fear of the almighty." This verse lets us know that in the eyes of Jesus, friendships are significant. The way we treat our friends and the way we develop our friendships will be the standard by which we are judged in the end. Scripture says after Job had prayed for his friends, the Lord restored his fortune and gave him twice as much as he had before (see Job 42:10). We miss the significance of this verse if we just take it to mean that God replaced everything Job had lost.

The verse says that *after Job had prayed for his friends*, the Lord restored his fortune and gave him twice as much as he had before because he was a good friend as evidenced by praying for his friends who had not treated him well during his ordeal. When you read the discourse between Job and his friends, they all pursued and shared their own rationale for Job's predicament. But Job did not throw them under the proverbial bus after he had his encounter with the Lord, but instead he prayed for them. This is the reason we need good friends and why we need to be a good friend. We should be praying for our friends because the Lord says that He hears the prayers of a righteous man (see Proverbs 15:29).

I recently felt the need to conduct the five-week men's group series on relationships because I was observing men who are saved by the blood but were treating their friendships as if they were worldly friendships. There's no faster way to divide the body of Christ than for friendships to fall apart. That's why it's always risky to start small groups where friendships are formed because as soon as they are formed, they can end because of some offense given or taken. After the series, our group has grown closer, and friendships are now treated with respect and reverence.

A friend will challenge you to step up higher, to go deeper, and to hang in there when needed. We should also be doing that for our friends. This is how we grow and how iron sharpens iron. Scripture says that two are better than one because if one falls, the other is there to lift him up. When we have the right friends, we are able to identify and resist the schemes of the enemy. We can stand when we have done everything to stand.

I love the picture of Aaron and Hur holding up Moses' hands during the battle. When Moses' hands came down, the Israelites would start to lose the battle; but when his hands stayed up as a symbol of intercession, the Israelites would start to win. So to ensure the victory, Aaron and Hur stood beside Moses and held up his hands (see Exodus 17:12). That's what friends do.

When we're tired of holding up our hands, they come beside us and hold up our hands for us. That's a powerful picture on what friendships looks like. As a man of God, we are called to be as wise as serpents and harmless as doves (see Matthew 10:16). This means we shouldn't be tyrants or self-serving in our actions and relationships but at the same time be wise in how we cultivate them. This is an important role in every man of God's life because the friends we chose will determine where we end up. Now I'm not saying to discard your current friends, but keep in mind bad company corrupts good character.

A wise man once told me that it's easier for someone to pull you down the mountain than it is for you to pull them up that same mountain. Some of you have been carrying some dead weight for a long time, and you wonder why you can't move forward. A good friend encourages us and supports us. In our role as a friend, it's our job to encourage and support the people we have chosen to have a friendship with.

I believe this is straight from the Holy Spirit. It's through our friendships that God is able to show Himself and make Himself available for others. It's because of my friendships that I have grown in the Lord and because of my friendship that I have seen others grow in the Lord. It's through our friendships that God receives glory through us and because of us.

I had the privilege of playing football at the semi-pro level, playing for a team called the Marlborough Shamrocks. We won five national championships and over a dozen league championships while I played for them. We had a talented group of guys on the team, but the real reason we were so successful was because we were all good friends. In fact, if you look around at all the championship teams at every level of any sport, you will see a group of men or woman who are close friends. I've also coached championship teams and again the common denominator is that they were all close friends.

It's special to go through something with a friend. The accomplishments seem so much better and greater and it strengthens the bond between them. I've not played football for a long time but I'm still friends with every man who played on that team in Marlborough, Massachusetts. A man of God will be evaluated by the company he keeps and how he treated the people around him.

A good friend in a man of God's life is a much needed commodity. We need to have good friends in our lives, and we need to be a good friend to others.

FINAL THOUGHT

When looking for examples of friends in the Bible I can't help but consider the disciples. Just think about it for a second. How can twelve men live and travel together for three and a half years and not kill each other? The only way they can do that is if they are truly friends. Jesus cultivated friends because these twelve would change the world.

This is a great example of how good friends together can change the world. I'm sure they had their differences but at the end of the day they supported each other. By the way, a good friend doesn't mean they agree with everything they do. In fact, a good friend should tell you when you're wrong. A good friend should help you get back on track when you're lost. The disciples were all good friends and a great example of what friendship looks like.

REFLECTION QUESTIONS

1. Are you a friend who can be counted on?
2. Do you value your friendships?
3. Do you have someone like Jonathan to call friend?
4. Are you the type of friend who encourages others?
5. If they were asked, how would your friends describe you as a friend?

ADDITIONAL REFERENCES

Job 6:14
Psalms 133:1
Ecclesiastes 4:9-10
Colossians 3:13
1 Thessalonians 5:11

Chapter 5

THE ROLE OF FATHER

"That was when the world wasn't so big, and I could see everywhere. It was when my father was a hero and not a human. "
– Markus Zusak

"I will guide you in the way of wisdom and I will lead you in upright paths. When you walk, your steps will not be hampered, and when you run, you will not stumble."
– Proverbs 4:11

The man of God plays many roles and one of the most important ones is the role of father. The father is so important to his family for many reasons which is why I wrote a book just about fathers. If you haven't read my book, *The Love of the Father*, please get a copy, but I'm not here to rewrite that book. *The Love of a Father* speaks more to the challenges of fatherhood, but this chapter will center on the role of the father. Granted, they do blend together, but I will try my best to stay focused.

We have a great example of what a good Father looks and acts like. The good Father loves unconditionally and bears wrongs with a strong heart. When I think of a good Father, my Heavenly Father comes to mind (my Abba). He's the great example as to what we should all be.

But I know you may dismiss this because He is God! Yes He is, but He has given us the ability to be good fathers as well. The role of the father is so important that our enemy has tried to take us out from the very beginning of creation. He disgraced Adam whose actions led to his eviction from the Garden of Eden. Our enemy caused Eve to eat the forbidden fruit and have Adam to also eat the fruit, which brought our sin nature into existence. Since that time, the enemy has sought to divide the family.

His strategy to split up the family is to take the fathers away. Without the father, the family is diminished. I am not taking anything away from our sisters, but God made man the head of the family as Christ is the head of the church. To be the head means to lead with integrity and love. It doesn't mean to lord it over a family, or to control and destroy families. It means to be the example of God in our families. As Paul said, "Follow me as I follow Christ" (1 Corinthians 11:1). We must say to our family members, "Follow me as I follow the Lord" and "As for me and my house we shall serve the Lord." This has to be the heart of the father in our families.

As a state trooper, I've seen the devastation caused by fathers who did not care about their families. It saddened me every time I saw it. We have no idea what it does to our children. If I gave you the stats on runaway kids or girls selling themselves into prostitution, you would be amazed. My book on fathers has the data for you to read.

Let's me give it to you straight: Fatherhood in America has been weighed and found wanting. Now don't get me wrong, for I know there are some outstanding fathers out there who are doing the job and doing it well. If you're one of those fathers, I salute you. Please keep doing what you're doing. At the end of this existence, we'll all be in God's big family. That's why we must learn our role as a father here on earth. That way we are prepared for what is to come, and so we can also teach our children to know how to relate to and accept our Father in heaven.

Here's the other problem with the lack of fathers. The father's role is to be like our Father in heaven. When earthly fathers function well, it is easier for their children to know and accept their heavenly Father. However, we make it difficult for our children to see God in heaven when we give them a poor likeness of Him. When our children do not know how to be fathered because they have never been fathered, then it becomes hard for them to receive from Father God.

You might read this and say to yourself, *I was never fathered so how am I to know how to father well?* If you are asking yourself that question, you are already in a better place. All you have to do now is ask your heavenly Father to come into your life and bring godly men into your life to help show you the ways of the Father.

If you've read my first book, you know I didn't have a good father role model growing up. Consequently, it was hard for me to see God as a Father who is always there and cares about me and what I care about. I struggled to know that there is a Father in heaven who is looking out for my best interests. That was a novel idea to me, that someone was looking out for my best interests. However, God brought several godly men into my life who showed me what the love of the Father looks like. Then the Father himself came into my life and blew me away with His love and acceptance.

I remember growing up watching television shows like *Father Knows Best* and *Wait 'til Your Father Gets Home*. Those shows aired when the father role was still significant in the family and depicted fathers who were close to ideal. Yet over time since then, the importance of the father in the family has diminished for many reasons.

I really could go on and on about this role because it is the call that is on my life: to encourage father's and men to be the best they can be. I do so because we don't truly know or see the importance of the many roles we play as men of God. Most of us just go about our days living the life we have been dealt, not putting much thought into the importance of the father role many of us have.

I consider my role as father to be just as important as my role as a pastor. As a pastor, God has placed lives in my hands and at the end of this, I'll answer to God for as to how I handled those He entrusted to me. It's the same with me as a father. I'm responsible for my children and will have to answer to God for how I handled fatherhood. The same is true for you, if you're a father. It's the most important role we will ever have. I know I've said that several times, but a mentor of mine said, "Tell them once, repeat it, and tell them again."

"To her, the name of father was another name for love." — Fanny Fern

I love this quote from Fanny Fern because my wish is that when my daughters think of love, they will think of me. This is how I think and feel when I consider my Father in heaven. He's the abundant, beneficent, beautiful, accepting (Abba) Father from above. We're truly blessed to be in His hands and under His watchful care.

We can struggle with our identity as fathers because some of us have not grown up in homes where our fathers showed their love for us in this way. Because of that, we have a distorted picture of fatherhood. But our Abba Father in Heaven is not only correcting the picture, but he *is* the picture of fatherhood. He is calling all men to be like Him.

He does this by making us like his son Jesus. As we become more like Jesus, we become more like our Father in heaven. Jesus Himself said that if we have seen Him then we have seen the Father. Jesus is the exact representation of our Father in Heaven, so if we are being made to be like Jesus then we are being made to be like our Father God.

As a man of God one of the roles that we may find ourselves playing is the role of the father. Like I said, if you do not have any biological children that is ok, because Abba will bring you into a situation where you become a spiritual father. Both the biological and the spiritual are vital and essential to the growth of the children of God.

FINAL THOUGHTS

As we look at the incident in the book of Genesis where Cain killed Abel, what is interesting is that Adam is nowhere to be found. He never commented on the murder of a son and brother. But we do see a good Father in the Garden. God tells Cain that sin is crouching like a lion waiting to devour him. God was warning him as to what can happen if he let his anger take hold of him.

Then after Cain killed his brother, it is God who confronted Cain. Yes, not Adam but God asked Cain where his brother was. Cain replied with his famous answer "Am I my brother's keeper?" What a lame answer, but God saw right through it. God told Cain that Abel's blood was crying out from the ground.

The final thing that God does with Cain is extend mercy to him. God would have been in the right just to kill Cain right there, but He didn't. Instead He sent Cain away from the place where they were living. He even put a mark on Cain so no one who found him would try and kill him. These are the deeds of a good father. I am not putting Adam down but let's face it: Adam dropped the ball where his family was concerned in this situation.

The love of the Father always shines through every situation. The love of the Father rebukes, shows mercy, and loves despite the issues and situations the children find themselves in. We see that behavior clearly in our Father God.

REFLECTION QUESTIONS

1. How much thought have you put into what a father should be?

2. Has your father played a significant role in your life? How so? Why or why not?

3. How can you be the best version of father-hood to your children?

4. Can you see how your Father in heaven has fathered you?

ADDITIONAL REFERENCES:

Psalm 103:13
Proverbs 4:11
Proverbs 23:24
Hebrews 12:7

Chapter 6

THE ROLE OF HUSBAND

"Being a good husband is like being a good stand-up comic. You need ten years before you can even call yourself a beginner."
– Jerry Seinfeld

"Likewise, husbands, live with your wives in an understanding way, showing honor to the woman as the weaker vessel, since they are heirs with you of the grace of life, so that your prayers may not be hindered."
– 1 Peter 3:7

"Husbands, love your wives, as Christ loved the church and gave himself up for her."
– Ephesians 5:25

You may think of skipping this chapter because you're not married. But I say that a wise man studies what he will do before he does it. If you're not married, this will still be a good chapter for you to read, for one day you may be and the time to prepare to be a good husband is not after you become one but before. So, I recommend you continue to read and glean what you can from the next few pages. If you are married, however, I pray this will give you strength and courage to be the husband you're called and always desired to be.

The Bible says much about the role of the husband. I can't say that I have always been a good husband. This is my second marriage, and I'm still striving to be the best husband I can be. But is it good enough? I know one thing to be true about my second marriage and it's that God is steering the ship of my life now and I'm a more godly husband now than I was in my youth.

As a man of God, one of our roles that can bring the most joy and happiness is to be a godly husband. God's Word says a man finds a good thing when he finds a good wife. In my wife Marissa, I have found a good thing. When we got married in the presence of God, vowing before God and witnesses to keep our marriage covenant, it was and still is a good thing.

However, we can ruin a good thing or underlive our marriage's potential in many cases. I know I violated the truth found in 1 Peter 3:7 in my first marriage. I didn't live with my then wife in an understanding way. I know now what that means and looks like, but I didn't in my younger day. Like when I was young, other men of God don't always live in an understanding way with our wives, and thus we find ourselves lost in a marriage.

The Lord says that we should love our wives as He has loved the church and gave Himself up for her. As men of God, we must cover and protect our families. This means loving our wives the same way Christ loved the church. I get it that this is easier said than done. This requires lots of prayer and reliance on Jesus as well as dying to self. That is why we are called sons of God, for we can call on Him to help and transform us into the loving husbands He wants us to be.

The problem often comes when we struggle in our marriages and try to fix them ourselves. We can't fix it because it's not that we have done wrong, it's that we are wrong. We are self-centered and often don't want anyone else's help to fix our problem. Only with the help of God can we even come close to who we should be, doing what we should do as husbands.

Ephesians 5:28 states, "In the same way husbands should love their wives as their own bodies. He who loves his wife loves himself." Why would Paul say this? As I started to do my research, I realized that in the very beginning in Genesis 1, God said, "Let's make them male and female, and for this reason a man shall leave his father and mother and join with his wife, and they shall become one flesh" (my paraphrase). Paul reiterated this command, when he wrote, "Therefore, a man shall leave his father and mother and hold fast to his wife, and the two shall become one flesh" (Ephesians 5:31).

This process of two becoming one flesh

represents the perfect image of God, for God is multiple persons but one and the marriage relationship mirrors that mystery. When the man and woman become one, they reflect the perfect image of God. That is why Paul was right when he wrote that he who loves his wife loves himself. I would also add that he who loves his wife loves God.

When Marissa and I met, I had no idea why God had brought us together. I remember praying, "Lord, if this woman is to be my friend that's fine. If she's to be my wife, that is fine. I will let You determine the outcome of this relationship." Little did I know that she would become my wife. She became the love of my life and literally saved it (my life) at the same time because of the new life I found as we became one flesh – and that one flesh reflected the image of God. I guess I do love myself because I love my wife. This is what the man of God does as a husband.

We're called to be the priest in our homes. We're commissioned to protect our families and to show them the way to the Lord. When we fail at this, we cause chaos in the lives of those around us. This I know because I was married once before, and I failed miserably. The marriage failed because I wasn't who I was supposed to be. I was not the priest or the protector. When the marriage ended, my daughter was lost for a time and the lives of my ex-wife and daughter were in chaos – chaos I created because I wasn't the husband I was supposed to be.

Thank God, He gave me another chance

at love. So, I can speak about his because I have had the experience of failing. I never want to talk and teach about issues and situations unless I've experienced them myself and I can speak to the issue of being a husband because it now commands all our attention to make our relationship all God wants it to be.

When we talk of coming together in body, mind, and soul, it means that we as men can no longer make decisions based on our own desires and needs. We must consider someone else in the equation. The role of the husband means I am no longer my own, but I belong to someone else. This is again similar to our relationship with Abba Father for we no longer have a claim on our lives for they now belong to God and are hidden in Him. As a husband, we become one flesh with our wives which means we no longer belong just to ourselves. We have a responsibility to our wives.

Now this is a ball that I totally dropped in my first marriage. I hope that I'm not dropping the ball in this marriage. The only way we can be sure not to drop the ball of responsibility is to love our wives as we love ourselves. Scripture says that Jesus gave Himself up for the Church. The Church is the bride of God, so in the same way we should be willing to give of ourselves for our wives. This is the role of the husband for the man of God. In return, we get love not just from our wives, but also from our Father in heaven. He smiles down on us and blesses our marriage.

I pray every day that the Lord will bless my marriage. I pray that the love of Jesus is the centerpiece of our relationship. I strive to honor my wife as I honor Jesus. If we're not praying for our wives, we are falling short of our role as priests in our families. We should also be praying for our children along with our wives. I try never to leave my house in the morning without praying for my wife and daughters. If you're not praying for God's protection over your family, you need to start right now.

Proverbs 18:22 states, "He who finds a wife finds what is good and receives favor from the Lord." We find favor from the Lord when we find a wife. You don't want to be married to someone who doesn't share your Kingdom values of righteous living. So if you're not married, pray and ask the Lord to lead you to the right woman. She has a vital role to play in your marriage as well as your calling. With God's right person behind you, the sky will literally be the limit for you.

Each one of these roles merits its own book. However, I'm attempting to give you a brief overview of the many roles that we play as sons of God. All the roles are of equal importance but the role of the husband should and does stand out amongst all the roles.

Of course, these roles don't exist in isolation. We're living them all simultaneously: father, husband, friend, etc. God wants us to be a consistent man of God in all our roles. I'll speak about this in more depth in a later chapter. But suffice it to say for now that we walk in many roles as men. We find ourselves in many different places where we have to show our true face in that moment.

I encourage you to let that face be the face that exudes and represents Jesus our Lord. As our brother and pastor Tony Evans said, "A husband's love is meant to be so powerful that it transforms his wife into what she should be, just as Christ's love for the church transforms us into what we should be."

FINAL THOUGHT

When I think of a husband in the Bible, I think of the minor prophet named Hosea. I know that God used the relationship between Hosea and his wife Gomer as an example of His marriage to Israel, but look at the dedication Hosea had. Also, look at the dedication and love that God has for Israel.

It is amazing to see that Gomer had committed prostitution as Israel had committed prostitution by worshiping other gods. Even though Israel committed spiritual adultery, God still loved Israel and still does today. This is a great story because He uses His prophet Hosea to show the nation their unfaithfulness through Gomer, Hosea's wife.

The pain that Hosea felt over his wife is the same pain God was feeling over Israel. It is the same pain He feels when we are not faithful to Him. Let's learn a lesson from the story of Hosea and Gomer. Let's look at the commitment and the devotion that was shown and let's love our wives in this way. God will honor you because this is how He unconditionally loves us.

REFLECTION QUESTIONS

1. Have you put much thought into your role as a husband?

2. Have you evaluated your performance as a husband?

3. What can you do to be a better husband, and when should you start?

4. Do you have any good models in your circle you can follow and consult with?

5. If you're not married but feel one day you may be, what can you do today to prepare for that important role?

ADDITIONAL REFERENCES:

Genesis 2:23-24
Malachi 2:15
Matthew 19:4-6
Mark 10:6-9
1 Corinthians 11:3

Chapter 7

THE ROLE OF MENTOR

"A mentor is someone who sees more talent and ability within you, than you see in yourself, and helps bring it out of you."
– Bob Proctor.

"Be shepherds of God's flock that is under your care, watching over them – not because you must, but because you are willing, as God wants you to be; not pursuing dishonest gain, but eager to serve; not lording it over those entrusted to you, but being examples to the flock."
– 1 Peter 5:2-3

Another role for the son or man of God will be that of a mentor. A mentor is an experienced person in a company, college, church, or school who trains and counsels employees, students, or disciples in some specific area of life or ministry. In the church, these are our spiritual fathers, mothers, pastors, and elders, but in truth, a mentor doesn't have to have a title or role.

It's just someone who others recognize as having a special skill or trait which others want to learn or develop. Thus they seek out this person to train and impart wisdom to them in areas like finances, public speaking, parenting, or any number of life skills and roles. In a sense, God calls all of us to be mentors, which means God places us in positions to help those He has called to perform some specific task or duty.

We should take this role seriously because souls are on the line. The people God calls us to mentor are expecting us to impart to them what God has given us for them. I remember once when I was a young pastor, my senior pastor sent out a video. The video was of someone speaking about the keys to her future that her pastor had. That video made quite an impact on me and I remember sending a message back telling my pastor that I wanted every key the Lord has given him for me.

God has entrusted keys to our calling in the hands of others, just like the one who has to train you on the job, just like the one who has to lead you on the team, and just like the one who must show you the system God has someone He has called to walk with us. That someone could be you.

The role of the mentor isn't to lord it over those God has joined or brought to us. Instead, we are to lead and instruct them. There are many examples of men serving as mentors for others in God's Word. Of course, Jesus would be the most prominent and successful mentor, for He chose twelve men, poured himself into them, and once they were filled with the Spirit, they went out and turned the world upside down.

Then there was the Apostle Paul choosing a young disciple named Timothy to travel with him:

> Paul came to Derbe and then to Lystra, where a disciple named Timothy lived, whose mother was Jewish and a believer but whose father was a Greek. The believers at Lystra and Iconium spoke well of him. Paul wanted to take him along on the journey, so he circumcised him because of the Jews who lived in that area, for they all knew that his father was a Greek. As they traveled from town to town, they delivered the decisions reached by the apostles and elders in Jerusalem for the people to obey. So the churches were strengthened in the faith and grew daily in numbers (Acts 16:1-5).

Anyone can see the nature of the relationship between these two men when they read Paul's two letters to Timothy. Paul imparted all that he had to his younger protégé and Timothy went on to be a great leader in his own right. In fact, Paul instructed Timothy to continue the process of mentoring others when he wrote,

> You then, my son, be strong in the grace that is in Christ Jesus. And the things you have heard me say in the

presence of many witnesses entrust to reliable people who will also be qualified to teach others (2 Timothy 2:1-2).

However, the story and relationship I would like to highlight is the one between the prophet Samuel and King David. Their relationship began when God directed Samuel to go and anoint the new king of Israel:

> The Lord said to Samuel, "How long will you mourn for Saul, since I have rejected him as king over Israel? Fill your horn with oil and be on your way; I am sending you to Jesse of Bethlehem. I have chosen one of his sons to be king."

> But Samuel said, "How can I go? If Saul hears about it, he will kill me."

> The Lord said, "Take a heifer with you and say, 'I have come to sacrifice to the Lord.' Invite Jesse to the sacrifice, and I will show you what to do. You are to anoint for me the one I indicate."

> Samuel did what the Lord said. When he arrived at Bethlehem, the elders of the town trembled when they met him. They asked, "Do you come in peace?"

> Samuel replied, "Yes, in peace; I have come to sacrifice to the Lord. Consecrate yourselves and come to the sacrifice with me." Then he consecrated Jesse and his sons and invited them to the sacrifice.

> When they arrived, Samuel saw Eliab and thought, "Surely the Lord's

anointed stands here before the Lord."

But the Lord said to Samuel, "Do not consider his appearance or his height, for I have rejected him. The Lord does not look at the things people look at. People look at the outward appearance, but the Lord looks at the heart."

Then Jesse called Abinadab and had him pass in front of Samuel. But Samuel said, "The Lord has not chosen this one either." Jesse then had Shammah pass by, but Samuel said, "Nor has the Lord chosen this one." Jesse had seven of his sons pass before Samuel, but Samuel said to him, "The Lord has not chosen these." So he asked Jesse, "Are these all the sons you have?"

"There is still the youngest," Jesse answered. "He is tending the sheep."

Samuel said, "Send for him; we will not sit down until he arrives."

So he sent for him and had him brought in. He was glowing with health and had a fine appearance and handsome features.

Then the Lord said, "Rise and anoint him; this is the one."

So Samuel took the horn of oil and anointed him in the presence of his brothers, and from that day on the Spirit of the Lord came powerfully upon David. Samuel then went to Ramah (1 Samuel 16:1-13).

In this account, we see that God had given Samuel the job of anointing David to be the next king of Israel. Samuel became David's mentor from that time on. We can see in later chapters that whenever David had questions or concerns, he would go to Samuel in Ramah. David was only about twelve years old when he was anointed to be king. What a responsibility that must have been for Samuel.

Anointing David wasn't just a one-time event for Samuel. Samuel had to become the mentor for the next king. I doubt if Samuel mentored David in the art of combat or tending sheep. He did mentor him, however, in how to hear from the Lord and also how to handle power in a way that was unlike how Saul did.

What I like about this passage is that Samuel does what God called him to do and no more. He didn't try to control David. He did not put a heavy yoke on David. The passage says that when Samuel anointed David, the Holy Spirit came upon him. So, if you're worried about whether or not you're capable of guiding the man or woman of God you're assigned to mentor, there's no need to so do. The Holy Spirit is involved and will help to guide them.

Later in the story, we see that when Saul was trying to kill David, he took refuge by going to Samuel in Ramah. It was in Ramah that David poured out his woes to the great prophet who had anointed him. The mentor is sometimes a shoulder to cry on. After this, David and Samuel went to Naioth to get away from Saul. Sometimes the mentor is a protector. It's interesting that when Saul heard that David was visiting with Samuel, he sent soldiers to arrest David, but the Lord caused them to prophesy and go back without David (see 1 Samuel 19:18-24).

Saul sent two more groups of soldiers and the same happened to all of them; they were unable to get to David. Finally, Saul went, and the same thing happened to him – he began to prophesy. That tells me that the Holy Spirit is not in it to help the mentor but the mentee. The mentor is in some sense a gatekeeper for the anointed, first providing insight into their purpose and then protecting them while they are preparing to fully engage their purpose. Samuel died before David ascended the throne but we can be sure that Samuel instructed David in what he should do once he became king. That's what a mentor looks like.

Believe it or not, Saul was also a mentor to David. How else would David know the intricacies of the king's court? He learned it from his time serving as Saul's armor bearer. Just like Moses learned how to lead people from Pharaoh, David learned from Saul. God uses people we would not think capable to mentor His anointed. In fact, Saul mentored David by providing a bad example of what godly leadership should be. Saul taught David how not to be a leader and David learned the lesson!

You may be reading this and think that the story of Samuel and David was about two unique men, but you are not anointed like they were. The word *anointed* simply means chosen. You have been chosen and those who God sends your way for you to mentor have been chosen. We see many mentors in the Bible because God always sends someone to help those He has called. You may have a small role or a big role, but the importance of the role is the same.

There's a saying that when the student is ready, the teacher will appear. I believe it's the same in reverse. When the teacher is ready, God will send a student. That means we as mentors should prepare ourselves to receive and train the Lord's anointed. I tell men in our Rally Point group every week that what they learn in our sessions isn't only for them, but also for someone else. We cannot hoard what the Lord has given us for He has given it to us for two reasons. The first is to grow and mature us, and the second is to give to someone God has called us to give it to.

Thus, the role of the mentor is one of extreme importance, and we should fulfill it with the utmost seriousness. God is depending on you and your charge is depending on you. You have the keys to help unlock someone's call and it's up to you to help them perfect and express their God-given purpose.

I wouldn't want to be the one who stands before Jesus having been given an assignment to mentor someone but failed. Or I wouldn't want to be someone who has mistreated or lorded their position over the person God has sent. This will take prayer and patience on the part of the mentor for this not to happen.

FINAL THOUGHTS

Let's look at the relationship between King Hezekiah and the prophet Isaiah.

> And his servants said still more against the Lord God and against his servant Hezekiah. And he wrote letters to cast contempt on the Lord, the God of Israel, and to speak against him, saying, "Like the gods of the nations of the lands who have not delivered their people from my hands, so the God of Hezekiah will not deliver his people from my hand." And they shouted it with a loud voice in the language of Judah to the people of Jerusalem who were on the wall, to frighten and terrify them, in order that they might take the city. And they spoke of the God of Jerusalem as they spoke of the gods of the peoples of the earth, which are the work of men's hands. Then Hezekiah the king and Isaiah the prophet, the son of Amoz, prayed because of this and cried to heaven. And the Lord sent an angel, who cut off all the mighty warriors and commanders and officers in the camp of the king of Assyria (2 Chronicles 32:16-21, ESV).

Hezekiah is one of my favorite kings of Israel. To give you some background on this passage in case you are not aware of it, the Assyrians were the world conquers of their time. No one had been able to defeat them in battle. The Assyrians were the dominant culture and the fear of them spread throughout the known world. The commander of the Assyrian army sent a letter that addressed the people of Jerusalem, informing them of his prowess and victories over the other gods of the land.

Hezekiah took the letters and brought them to his mentor, Isaiah the prophet. Isaiah prayed with Hezekiah. This is a powerful picture of the mentor. One of the roles of the mentor, and I would go as far as to say probably the most important role, is to teach them how to pray. King Hezekiah would forever be able to say that he and his mentor prayed. God heard the prayers of the two men of God and answered. I would encourage you to read the story yourself, because this is another great example of the mentor and mentee relationship. The Bible is full of them if you have the eyes to see them.

REFLECTION QUESTIONS

1. Think through what the role of the mentor is. Are you willing to step into and serve in that role?
2. Have you had a mentor(s) in your life? What did they impart to you?
3. How did Samuel mentor David?
4. Are there any other mentors in the Bible who you can learn from?

ADDITIONAL REFERENCES

Psalm 71:18
Proverbs 1:5
Proverbs 9:9
Proverbs 27:17
1 Thessalonians 2:8

Chapter 8

THE ROLE OF LEADER

Before you are a leader, success is all about growing yourself. When you become a leader, success is all about growing others.
– Jack Welch

A leader is a dealer in hope.
– Napoleon Bonaparte

"It shall not be so among you. But whoever would be great among you must be your servant, and whoever would be first among you must be your slave, even as the Son of Man came not to be served but to serve, and to give his life as a ransom for many."
– Matthew 20:26-28

The man of God will be called to lead because leadership is important to God. He is the one who promotes one and puts down another as we are told in Psalm 75. But godly leadership is completely different than what the world has made leadership to be. Leadership in the Kingdom of God means coming under authority, instead of lording one's authority over others. Leadership is about gaining influence that emanates from relationships with the people who are following. Simply put, Jesus equates leadership with service.

As a student in high school, I strove to be a leader but not for the right reasons. Sometimes I was a leader because at times I was the best athlete. At others times, I was the leader because I was the loudest. I now realize that being a leader is much more than that. It's not about being in the spotlight or feeding one's ego. Leaders have responsibilities before God as people who impact the lives of others.

When I was in the army, I was stationed in the 82nd Airborne Division when I was sent to Desert Shield and then Desert Storm. I was in field artillery and my unit was attached to an infantry unit. The leader of that division was a man by the name of General Johnson. The first thing I realized was that the men in the infantry unit loved him and at first I didn't know why.

Then one day I was assigned to guard duty at the entrance to our base. This meant checking vehicles and people who were coming into and out of the base. After a few hours on duty, I noticed this man coming over to me with stars on his helmet. I saluted him and he identified himself as General Johnson. He never asked me what my assignment was or if I had any issues. He asked how I was doing and how my family was back at home. I instantly understood why his soldiers loved him so much.

Although he had a big mission to accomplish and was responsible for a lot of soldiers and decisions, he was still concerned about those people under him. That is a great picture of a good leader. I vowed I would be like that even in my small sphere of influence. To be honest, that was the first time I really considered what it meant to be a leader and I concluded that being a leader was about having relationships with those around you. Leadership is about making other people better as a result of your presence and making sure that the impact lasts in your absence. I've been fortunate to have some good leaders in my life.

Here's another thing about being a leader. If you're leading, you should be leading someone but also should be led by someone. You should never stop being a student of leadership even as you are leading.

As a football coach for West Warwick High School, I lead many young men and coaches. The good thing about being a leader is that it makes you have to walk out what you're trying to instill and teach. A key component of leadership is that you are what you preach. When we are what we preach, we are able to disciple those who are on our team and connected to our mission.

As a coach, one of my strengths is being able to see where someone might fit. Most coaches come in looking to do what they want to do, but the most effective coaches who are also leaders look and see what their team can do best. So I'm not so locked into what I want to do more so than what my team can do. That means putting my players in the right situations and allowing them to thrive in who they are and what their talents can provide.

But if I'm leading those on my team, it's so they then can take what I have done and make it better. A leader isn't afraid or intimidated by others who may outshine or one day take their place. The reason why the leader isn't worried is because if they are leading others properly, then the new leaders are an extension of that leader.

I've had some great leaders and some bad ones, which has taught me that we can learn from anyone who is in leadership if we have a heart to grow. Even the bad leader does some good things that we can take away and add to who we are as we saw in the relationship between Saul and David. Saul was a bad leader and taught David what not to do when he became king.

Leadership is influencing others to do what is needed to be done. We gain influence by building relationships. Do you think that after my conversation with General Johnson I would have done anything he asked me to do? I would because I knew I was valued and therefore, I then valued the mission.

We earn influence through building strong and credible relationships to then get those who are on our team to work together in one accord. My players and those I'm in charge of need to know they can contact me anytime of the day or night and I'll be there, and what they need does not have to only be about football.

Being a leader can be stressful which is why we need to have healthy outlets in order for us to be able to unwind. As our teams should be diversified, so should our activities outside the entity we are leading. I'm a football coach, a pastor, and a retired sergeant with the state police, but the thing that allows me to be flexible is what I do outside of my work. I have a YouTube channel called *Wes's Smokehouse BBQ*. I love BBQ and I love to make it. It takes me away from my stresses and anxiety of the things I'm responsible for. I'm also an author, having published my first book in December 2021 and my second book in 2022.

A leader needs to take periods of rest and relaxation to allow their mind to relax and stir up their creative juices. It is important to have other things in your life to occupy your time besides work. This allows you to stay mentally strong, energetic, and allows you to be more creative in your thinking as well. If you build your life around the thing that you're leading, you will burn out and not be effective for anyone.

Never Give Up

"I've missed more than 9000 shots in my career. I've lost almost 300 games. 26 times I've been trusted to take the game winning shot and missed. I've failed over and over and over again in my life. And that is why I succeed." – Michael Jordan

Michael Jordan will go down as one of the greatest basketball players of all time. He was also a great leader because he never quit. He picked himself up when he failed and tried again. A leader may fail but a good leader will never quit. They will continue to work hard to accomplish their goals. I call it the bounce back, for a good leader has the ability to bounce back from failure. A leader knows failure does not identify who they are, but quitting can: "For though the righteous fall seven times, they rise again, but the wicked stumble when calamity strikes" (Proverbs 24:16).

I know I've spoken about some great leaders, but the greatest of them all is Christ Jesus. What a picture He is of servant leadership. Jesus was 100% God and 100% man, yet He came to serve and pay a ransom for our freedom that we could never pray or repay. He could have called down legions of angels at any minute to defend His honor and escape His cross. Yet He was strength under control. He was power reigned in. He was a calm amidst the storm.

As a leader, He encouraged and empowered those around Him. Even on the cross as His accusers were calling Him names and ridiculing Him, yet He asked the Father to forgive them for they knew not what they were doing. That's a leader putting the people's needs before His own. The son of God was a humble servant as a leader and He now requires that His leaders follow His example:

> "Not so with you. Instead, whoever wants to become great among you must be your servant, and whoever wants to be first must be your slave—just as the

Son of Man did not come to be served, but to serve, and to give his life as a ransom for many" (Matthew 20:26-28).

In this passage, Jesus was telling His disciples that the greatest must be the least. He came to serve so we must serve as well. As a leader, I have to put my trust and faith in something or someone, so I choose to do so by following Christ. By doing so, my faith keeps me grounded in reality and the needs of others as well as approachable and teachable.

My faith also gives me direction. No one wants to follow someone who doesn't know where they're going. A leader must have direction and purpose. When a leader knows their calling in the Lord, it becomes easier to lead those God has called them to lead. When the man of God is called to be a leader we should take it seriously because it is a high calling.

FINAL THOUGHT

A great leader is someone who is led by God. We see so many great leaders in the Bible, but Moses stands out to me. When you look at Moses, you see someone who was thrown into the middle of a struggle.

> Then Moses went up from the plains of Moab to Mount Nebo, to the top of Pisgah, which is opposite Jericho. And the Lord showed him all the land, Gilead as far as Dan, all Naphtali, the land of Ephraim and Manasseh, all the land of Judah as far as the western sea, the Negeb, and the Plain, that is, the Valley of Jericho the city of palm trees, as far as Zoar. And the Lord said to him, "This is the land of which I swore to Abraham, to Isaac, and to Jacob, 'I will give it to your offspring.' I have let you see it with your eyes, but you shall not go over there."
>
> So Moses the servant of the Lord died there in the land of Moab, according to the word of the Lord, and he buried him in the valley in the land of Moab opposite Beth-peor; but no one knows the place of his burial to this day. Moses was 120 years old when he died. His eye was undimmed, and his vigor unabated. And the people of Israel wept for Moses in the plains of Moab thirty days. Then the days of weeping and mourning for Moses were ended (Deuteronomy 34:1-8, ESV).

It might seem strange to share the passage that describes Moses' death, but in a sense, this was the pinnacle for Moses. After leading the Hebrews for many years, Moses was at his end. Even though he didn't get to go into the Promised Land, God gave Moses a chance to see it. He saw it before any of the Hebrews saw it.

Moses is a great example of leadership. He does everything I have spoken about up to this point. Moses was a leader who was led by God. He trained up his successor. Moses treated the people fairly and didn't lord it over them. Moses handled disputes and even though he was angry because Israel had failed God, he continued to lead. Moses is known as a friend of God. Nowhere in Scripture do we see that God was this close with another man.

God showed himself to Moses and Moses spoke to God as a man speaks to a friend. Moses was in the presence of God more than anyone I can find in the Bible. He would have to hide his face because it would be so radiant after being in the presence of God.

If there is one word that exemplifies Moses' leadership, it would be humility. Moses was the most humble man on the earth. This tells us something of the need for leaders to be humble. Only then can God use the leader in the way they should go. When the leader is humble before the Lord, we see the power of God move through their life. I pray you model your leadership style after Moses.

REFLECTION QUESTIONS

1. Who were or are the good leaders in your life?
2. Can you name some great leaders in the Bible?
3. Have you been called a leader? In what settings?
4. What is your strongest virtue in leadership?

ADDITIONAL REFERENCES

Isaiah 41:10
Galatians 6:9
Hebrews 13:7
James 1:12

Chapter 9

ALL IN ONE

I know my rightful place as a child of God;
I am blessed and highly favored.
I am protected and delivered from every evil.
I am redeem and set free from
all bondages in Jesus' name.
– Lailah Gifty Akita, *Think Great: Be Great!*

"And not only this, but also, we ourselves,
having the first fruits of the Spirit, even we
ourselves groan within ourselves, waiting
eagerly for our adoption as sons, the
redemption of our body." – Romans 8:23

I've broken down the many different roles that we play as men of God. I'm sure if we took a deep dive, we could list a few more roles that we play. But here's a revelation that I received one day about the roles we play. I was breaking down our Rally Point core virtues. As I was dividing and studying them, I realized they are all working in me at the same time. So even though I took each role and looked at it individually, I often play or fulfill these many roles simultaneously. It's like having an orange and slicing it into nine slices. Even though the orange was sliced and separated, it would still be from the same orange.

My prayer every day is that God makes me the same man of God in all my roles, consistent in behavior and attitude. I don't want people wondering which Wes is going to show up. I want to be the man of God representing Him accurately in all I do. We have a great example of the perfect man of God in Jesus Christ who was consistently righteous, kind, gracious, and trustworthy. He was the same person in every role He had. I will speak more n Jesus in this and the next chapter, because He is the perfect example for us to look at. He is our model for life as men of God.

As a son, brother, and friend Jesus was the same Son of God and man of God in each instance. He never changed faces according to who He was with or what He was doing. We often morph into the person we need to be or are expected to be for the situation we find ourselves in. The truth is, God did not make us that way. If I'm different at work than I am at church, then there's a problem, and there's an imposter taking up one of the roles. God didn't create us to be or act differently in the various roles that we play as men.

Maybe the mistake I have made and that some others make is I used the word to *play* in connection role which sounds like we are acting. We should not be acting our way through life; we should be authentic. God has made you for a purpose and you have been designed to fulfill that purpose, It's something only you can do. Jesus never behaved differently with Peter than He did with Mary. He was the same person inside and out, in good times and bad. He was not hesitant to express who He was.

Maybe that's where we stumble. We're self-conscious and sometimes ashamed of who we really are. Once we start to accept who we really are is when we find true freedom. Once we get past our need or desire to be accepted by people and start to develop a reliance on Jesus Christ as our focus, then we are well on our way to being and not acting.

I was a Rhode Island state trooper for over 28 years. At the beginning of my career, I tried to be all things for all people and found myself failing in most of the things I was doing. It was not until I was well into my career when Jesus took hold of my heart. Once that happened, I started to work for Him and not for my colonel or my supervisor. My goal was to please Jesus and not try to please everyone else – including myself. Believe it or not, once I changed my focus to Jesus instead of my bosses, I started getting promotions.

Good things started to happen to me at work and I was recognized for who I was, not who I was pretending or trying to be. I discovered that people actually liked Wesley Pennington, the son of God, instead the Wesley Pennington who was trying to please everyone – and was pleasing no one. That is when I started to be the true me in all I was doing.

I accepted that God made me into His

son, that God has done a work in me and is still doing a work in me. To be honest, it takes too much work to try and please everyone. Jesus said, "My yoke is easy and my burden is light" and it really is. There's no one better to look to than Jesus as the real man of God in every and any situation and circumstance.

> When all things are subjected to him, then the Son Himself will also be subjected under Him who put all things in subjection under him, that God may be all in all (1 Corinthians 15:28).

This verse perfectly explains what I have taken nine chapters to try and clarify. God wants to be in all things – in you and in all that you do and in everything you put your hands to. Jesus was subject to God the Father and came under Him so that all things may be subjected to the Father, who is the one who made all things. In other words, we are being made daily into the image of Jesus. This means that as we are being transformed into His image – we are being subjected to His will.

If we're subjected to His will, then we must be who He has called us to be. That means we have to be consistent in all we do just like Jesus was. By doing so, we give God the glory in all that we do in our lives. That little bit of information right there alone was well worth the price of this book. John described Jesus when he wrote, "And the word became flesh and dwelt among us. And we saw His glory, glory as of grace and truth" (John 1:14). I'm getting excited just writing this. I hope you are by reading it as well.

I remember when a few of my pastor friends and I went go to Bishop T.D. Jakes men's conferences. Every once in a while, I would see someone just stand up and start running around the sanctuary. I always wondered what made him run like that. But as I write this, I have an urge to run around my living room. My wife would probably look at me like I am crazy, but the truth is, I am crazy – crazy for my Lord and Savior Jesus. Jesus is our great example of what a man of God should look like in all areas of life.

My brother, I thought it I was being present when I tried to be all things for all people. To my childhood friends, I was Wes the jokester. To my college friends, I was Wes the party animal. To my law enforcement friends, I was Wes the crazy guy. To my church friends, I was Wes the son of God. The problem was, I was only around my church friends every once in a while. So being honest, I was being everything else most of the time and the son of God only a little of the time. It does not work, and the result was I hurt some people and disappointed others.

I remember picturing that my worldly man was a 500-pound gorilla, and the godly man was an infant. The godly man was incapable of taking on and overcoming that 500-pound gorilla. I would pray for the Lord to help me overcome this giant in my life to no avail, because I was feeding the giant and starving my spiritual being.

Then one day God showed me in His mercy and grace that the battle was already won – if

I would accept and learn to live in the victory. As I allowed Jesus to make me more like Him, I started to see the transformation of the infant. I started to see the infant in me get stronger and braver. At first I didn't know it, but Jesus had started a transformation in me. If you want to know more about the transformation process, get a copy of my book *Through the Smoker.*

Eventually, I realized that the 500-pound gorilla was not so big and intimidating after all. It is like when we were in elementary, and the school yard bully looked so big until we grew and they did not seem so big after all. This was the revelation I received during my time of transformation. As I became more like Jesus, my God man grew and took control of my life. Today, the gorilla is the size of monkey – a small one at that.

I had gotten to the point where the one thing I wanted to do in my life, which was to be a trooper, had become a curse instead of a blessing. God had blessed me to become what I had always wanted in my life, but because I was trying to be all things to all people, I was failing. I was watching my fellow police academy classmates pass me by on the career ladder. I found myself all alone and with no one who really cared. At that time in my life, I made the decision to work as a trooper for God and not for man. Only then did being a trooper really become a blessing to me and my family. This is what happens when we try to be all things to all people.

Once I started to work for the Lord, allowing Him to be my guide and compass, people started to see me as Wesley Pennington – the real one, not the imposter or actor. I had tried for so long to get promoted and gain recognition, but it was not until I started to work for the Lord that the promotions and the recognition started to come. When I let my yes be yes and my no be no, God created character in me. I suddenly wanted to be a man of God in *all* aspects of my life, just like Jesus is. Because I was becoming more like Him, I was gaining control of my life – or should I say He was gaining control in me over every area.

I hope you didn't miss what I just wrote. You may think that in order to get control of your life, you need to work harder. You may think you need to be more disciplined. You may assume you must make the right connections with people. But if you notice, it wasn't until I surrendered to Jesus that I gained control. I gained control by giving up control and then started to become the one man of God in all the areas of my life. Stop trying to please everyone and just start pleasing Jesus.

You might be shaking your head right now, not convinced of the truth I just shared, but do me and yourself a favor. Just start trusting Him and watch what happens. See if your life doesn't start to change. And what's more, as He changes you, the benefits of being closer to and more like Him outweigh any of the other blessings.

The truth is we were created to be the singular person God called us to be. In fact, it's where we get the word integrity, which means wholeness or consistent. When we

have integrity, we are the same in every situation – steadfast, honest, empathetic, bold, and
straightforward. His Word says even as He
chose us to be in Him before the foundation
of the world, we should be holy and blameless
before him in love (see Ephesians 1:4). Because
of that, there will be no condemnation for those
who believe in Jesus Christ (see Romans 8:1).

FINAL THOUGHT

Josiah was eight years old when he began to reign, and he reigned thirty-one years in Jerusalem. And he did what was right in the eyes of the Lord, and walked in the ways of David his father; and he did not turn aside to the right hand or to the left. For in the eighth year of his reign, while he was yet a boy, he began to seek the God of David his father, and in the twelfth year he began to purge Judah and Jerusalem of the high places, the Asherim, and the carved and the metal images. And they chopped down the altars of the Baals in his presence, and he cut down the incense altars that stood above them. And he broke in pieces the Asherim and the carved and the metal images, and he made dust of them and scattered it over the graves of those who had sacrificed to them. He also burned the bones of the priests on their altars and cleansed Judah and Jerusalem. And in the cities of Manasseh, Ephraim, and Simeon, and as far as Naphtali, in their ruins all around, he broke down the altars and beat the Asherim and the images into powder and cut down all the incense altars throughout all the land of Israel. Then he returned to Jerusalem (2 Chronicles 34:1-7, ESV).

There are so many men in the Bible who could be mentioned here, but I chose Josiah.

Josiah was the king of Judah from approximately 640 to 609 B.C. His reign in Jerusalem is discussed in 2 Kings and 2 Chronicles. Josiah was the son of King Amon and the grandson of King Manasseh, both of whom were wicked kings of Judah. Yet Josiah was a godly king, even though he was one of the world's youngest kings. He began his reign at age eight after his father was assassinated. A highlight of Josiah's reign was his rediscovery of the Law of the Lord.

Second Kings 22:2 introduces Josiah by saying,

> And he did what was right in the eyes of the LORD and walked in all the way of David his father, and he did not turn aside to the right or to the left. In the eighteenth year of his reign, he raised money to repair the temple, and during the repairs the high priest Kilkiah found the Book of the Law. When Shapan the secretary read it to Josiah, the king tore his clothes, a sign of mourning and repentance (2 Kings 22:10-11).

King Josiah called for a time of national repentance. The Law was read to the people of the land, and a covenant made between the people and the Lord. Now if this is not a man of God in all he did, who is? Josiah is one of my favorite kings to study because he was a true man of God.

REFLECTION QUESTIONS

1. How big is your worldly man compared to your godly man?
2. What roles do you see you have in your life right now?
3. What kind of person do your friends, family, co-workers, and church family see you as?
4. What can you do to be the singular man of God in every and any situation and role?

ADDITIONAL REFERENCES

Isaiah 41:10
1 Corinthians 16:13
Philippians 2:8
1 Timothy 6:11
James 1:13

Chapter 10

SOME GOOD ROLE MODELS

"I take pride in being the same person."
– President Gorge W. Bush

*"'Teacher, which is the greatest
commandment in the Law?' Jesus replied:
'Love the Lord your God with all your
heart and with all your soul and with all
your mind.' This is the first and greatest
commandment. And the second is like it:
'Love your neighbor as yourself.' All the
Law and the Prophets hang on these two
commandments."* – Matthew 22:36-40

The second greatest command is to love
your neighbor as yourself. What is significant
about this is that Jesus said all the law and the
prophets hang on these two commandments.
Can I share with you a startling revelation?
When we allow Jesus to transform us into His
likeness, we are loving the Lord with all our

heart, mind, and strength. If we didn't love the Lord, we wouldn't allow this process to take place. And then as we're being made into the likeness of Jesus, we're becoming one man in all we are and do. The one man automatically and unconsciously fulfills the second greatest commandment.

Because Jesus is in us, we start to become more like Him through the work of the Spirit and then we naturally start to walk in our purpose while learning to love others as we love ourselves. I mentioned earlier that Jesus' yoke is easy and His burden is light, but sometimes it doesn't seem that way. Conforming to His image seems long and the path difficult.

However, it all begins by surrendering who we think we are to Jesus, so He can make us into who He called us to be. At the end of our journey, Jesus is the beginning and the end to who we are and who we are called to be. The key to unlocking our potential and purpose lies with Jesus and when it comes right down to it, who is better to be in charge of it? Jesus is the one perfect man so who better to make us perfect?

I was counseling a brother recently who had some big decisions to make. My advice to him was to be the man of God no matter what decision he made. I explained that if he's willing to be the man of God in every situations, then he couldn't miss. God would direct his steps and fulfill what we read in Philippians 2:12-13:

> Work hard to show the results of your salvation, obeying God with deep reverence and fear. For God is working in

you, giving you the desire and the power to do what pleases him.

Look at those verses again. God is working in us to give us the desire to do His will, and then when we commit to do it, He gives us to power to follow through. What a deal that is! It's God at the beginning and at the end, as well as throughout our pilgrimage. If our heart is to do God's will, we'll inevitably do and make the right decisions. At the very least, God will work things out for our benefit. I mentioned in an earlier chapter to let your yes be yes and your no be no (see Matthew 5:37). For me this was the beginning of the building of my character, and the beginning of my journey to be the man of God I'm called to be.

I'm not saying I've made it; I'm a work in progress just like you. I'm simply sharing some information I received from my own process. I see so many of my brothers struggling with who they are, and making many mistakes along the way. Not that we still won't make mistakes, but our mistakes won't be as disastrous when we're consistent and walk in the integrity of who each one of us is. None of us will be perfected until the day we meet Jesus or the day He returns.

What an amazing God we serve that He is continually making a way for us to be all we can be. I'm not sure how old you are but I remember a commercial when I was younger that was put out by the U.S. Army which said, "Be all you can be." The Army makes its soldiers all they can be through hard work and rigorous training, but Jesus does it through transformation. All you have to do is surrender and walk In His ways.

I guess I could summarize this book in just a few words: "Be all you can be by being the one man of God He created you to be." The book could have started and ended there, but I have a problem with such general, open-ended statements because they do not tell you the why or the how. They may inspire us, but they also leave us confused and lost, eventually walking away and quitting. That's why I felt it necessary to write about the different roles we play as sons of God: son, brother, friend, father, husband, mentor, and leader are but a few. We play many roles often at the same time.

For example, if you're having dinner with your family, you're probably playing the role of the father and the husband at the same time. You can be the friend and the mentor at the same time. But each role has its own intricacies and if we are not careful, we could find ourselves changing faces to meet each role – instead of having our one man "game face" on for each.

Simply let your yes be yes and your no be no. This is the beginning of becoming a consistent man of God in all you do. This is how you love your neighbor, and this is how you become an obedient son of God. The passage I included at the beginning this chapter says that all of the law and all of the prophets hang on these two commandments. That's amazingly simple but profound, if we take a second to look at it.

All of the Old Testament law rests on

whether or not you love God with all your mind, strength and soul, and then also love your neighbor as yourself. When you do this, you are satisfying what everyone believes is unsatisfiable and please God in ways that others will believe is too simple – for religion loves rules to follow. I'm sure you have heard that the law leads to death because we are all law-breakers and "the wages of sin is death" (see Romans 6:23).

Yet God did what no one thought could happen. He took what would bring death and caused it instead to bring life. The only way the law won't bring death is for someone to believe in Jesus. By believing in Jesus, every person can fulfill the essence of the Law outlined in those two commands by the filling of the Holy Spirit because then you or anyone else can love God with all your strength, mind, and soul, while also loving your neighbor.

The transformational process that starts upon our conversion makes you like Jesus and then, and only then, do you become the man you are called to be. This empowers you to grow closer to God your Father by becoming more like Jesus every day. As you become more like Him, you cannot help but love like He does.

That's the reason Jesus said that He didn't come to abolish the Law but to fulfill it, and in so doing He gave us the key to life. There's a three-part process involved in this key to life. First, we surrender our lives to Jesus Christ. Second, we welcome the Spirit of God to reside in us and allow Him to change us, for a life that is not changed is not a life surrendered. The third and final step is to be obedient and live out a life exhibiting the holiness of Jesus Christ.

The result of this process is, you guessed it, becoming the one man of God you're called to be, culminating in being perfected by Jesus and being welcomed into the presence of God. At that time, you will hear those thrilling words we all desire to hear:

> "His master replied, 'Well done, good and faithful servant! You have been faithful with a few things; I will put you in charge of many things. Come and share your master's happiness!'" (Matthew 25:23).

As if that isn't already fantastic, it gets better. Because we surrendered, having a changed life due to being obedient, in the end when the Master comes back, we will have invested our talents and multiplied them. It is then that we will hear the words "well done." I hope I've shown you how this all connects.

In my life, I've had to go through this process, and I'm still going through it. I was so far away from being the man of God that I would have thought I could never even come close to that lofty objective. I'm not saying I've succeeded or that Jesus has fully finished the work in me, but I have seen the difference as I live a life changed. Like I said in an earlier chapter, the 500-pound gorilla is now the baby and the man of God in me has become the 500-pound man.

Of course, I don't mean in actual weight

but in the size and significance of my heart, mind, and spirit. If you've read any of my books or followed me, you know my past. I went through a divorce, I was a dead-beat dad, and a failure at work. I was the lowest of them all. But with Jesus in my life everything has changed.

I've now been married for nine years and we're very happy. My relationship with my daughters is the best it's ever been, and I retired in 2022 after a little more than 28 years as a state policeman. I credit all those statistics and accomplishments to Jesus! He really is the author and creator of my life, and He has changed it in every way.

Like I have said previously, I'm no one special – just another son. That means if Jesus did it for me, He can and will do it for you. All it takes is a surrendered heart and a willingness to follow. If you need help with this, become a part of my Rally Point Ministry. Our core beliefs and virtues are listed at the end of this book.

Contact us online or request me to come and speak to your fellowship. I want to see all men have their lives transformed so they can become who they have been called to be. The affirmation we often make in church is true: "God is good all the time and all the time God is good." He is faithful. Simply put, my brother, it's all about Jesus and His love.

Bless you, and may the *ruach* of God empower your life with every breath to serve your God who fills you with the breath of life.

LET'S PRAY!

Oh Father, we sometimes forget about or neglect the power You've placed within us through your Spirit, and even more often, we forget that You've equipped us to use it for Your glory! Help us today – right here, right now – to speak to the dry bones within us and call ourselves to come to life so we may be ready, willing, and able to speak forth life and resurrection in Your name to others. Thank You for trusting us and inviting us to share in this incredible work. In Jesus' name, we pray. Amen.

REFLECTION QUESTIONS

1. Are you willing to surrender your heart to Jesus today?
2. Has your life been changed by the indwelling of the Holy Spirit? In what ways?
3. Are you willing to live a life of obedience for Jesus Christ?
4. Has your life been an example of a changed life from Jesus? If not, why not?

ADDITIONAL REFERENCES

Matthew 5:37
Matthew 22:36-40
Matthew 25:21

Chapter II

A FINAL
FINAL THOUGHT

*"The mark of a man of God is
God upon the man."* – Paul Washer

*"To be safe from the devil's snares, the
man of God must be completely obedient
to the Word of the Lord. The driver on the
highway is safe, not when he reads the signs
but when he obeys them."* – Unknown

I know I've been discussing how to look
to Jesus who is the perfect example of the one-
man concept, but let's look at some other men
of the Bible from whom we can learn a lot
about being a man of God.

1. Simon of Cyrene

Simon of Cyrene is well-known as the
man the Roman soldiers forced to help Jesus
carry His cross:

> And they forced a certain man who
> was passing by, Simon of Cyrene (the
> father of Alexander and Rufus), who
> was coming from the country, to car-
> ry his cross. And they brought him to

the place Golgotha (which is translated "Place of a Skull") (Mark 15:21-22 LEB).

Little did these soldiers know that they were immortalizing this man when they picked him out of a crowd and forced him to help Jesus! Do you know that when we meet Jesus, in a sense we are also made immortal? Jesus said to rejoice that your name is forever to be remembered because it's written in the book of life (see Luke 10:20). What a strange fate for Simon as described in the gospel narrative, who for an instant came into contact with Jesus Christ like two ships passing through the night, only to realize it was meant to be.

Simon was a Cyrenian – that is, he was a Jew by descent, probably born around and certainly a resident for purposes of commerce in Cyrene on the North African coast of the Mediterranean. No doubt he had come up to Jerusalem for the Passover, and like many of the strangers who flocked to the Holy City for the feast, he perhaps met some difficulty in finding accommodation in the city. Therefore, he was obliged to go to lodge in one of the outlying villages.

From this lodging, he was coming into the city in the morning, knowing nothing about Christ or His trial – knowing nothing of who he was about to meet. He then happened to see the procession as it was passing out of the gate. He was pressed into service by a centurion to help the fainting Christ carry the heavy cross. He probably thought Jesus a common criminal, and would certainly resent the task laid upon him by the gruff and unrelenting authority of the officer in command.

Yet Simon was gradually moved to sympathy as he drew closer and closer to the meekness of this prisoner, realizing that He was no ordinary prisoner or criminal. Finally, Simon yielded to the soul-conquering power of Christ. What we do know and can confirm is that Simon from this encounter became a strong man of God. How do we know? Let's examine our next character.

2. Rufus

A certain man from Cyrene, Simon, the father of *Alexander and Rufus*, was passing by on his way in from the country, and they forced him to carry the cross (Mark 15:21).

Greet *Rufus*, chosen in the Lord, and his mother, who has been a mother to me, too (Romans 16:13).

Both of the sons of Simon, Alexander and Rufus, gained renown in Christianity in the first century. If the sons of Simon became sons of God, that would mean the encounter with Jesus did more for Simon than is written. Just like us, Simon was changed with one look into the eyes of Jesus. Even though he's not mentioned further in the Bible, we can see the effects of his life through his sons. If the only legacy we leave on this planet is that our children are well known in their Christian walk, then we will have left a great inheritance.

3. Boaz

Then Boaz announced to the elders and all the people, "Today you are witnesses that I have bought from Naomi all the property of Elimelek, Kilion and Mahlon. I have also acquired Ruth the Moabite, Mahlon's widow, as my wife, in order to maintain the name of the dead with his property, so that his name will not disappear from among his family or from his hometown. Today you are witnesses!" (Ruth 4:9-10).

In my opinion, Boaz is a perfect example of the man of God in all that he did. If you're not familiar with the story of Ruth and Naomi, it's worth reading the book of Ruth. This makes for fascinating reading also because Boaz and Ruth are listed in Jesus' family tree. My abridged version of his story is as follows.

Naomi was married and had two sons. Her family left Bethlehem and went to the land of Canaan where her two sons met and married local Moabite women. One of the women's names was Ruth. Soon, however, calamity struck Naomi and her family when her husband and both her sons died. Since life was hard, she decided to go back to Bethlehem, the place of her heritage. Out of the two daughters-in-law, Ruth, was the only one who refused to stay behind in her homeland but instead went back with Naomi to Bethlehem

Once back in Naomi's hometown, they were without food or provision. One day, Ruth went into a field to glean after the wheat pickers had been through when Boaz noticed Ruth. Truthfully, I could have written this entire chapter on Boaz because he did everything right where Ruth is concerned.

First, he could have forced her to leave his field once he saw her in a sense trespassing, but he did not. Instead he instructed the pickers the leave some of the good portions of the harvest for Ruth to find. He also directed them not to harm her and to watch out for her. When Ruth told this to Naomi, Naomi informed Ruth that Boaz was a distant relative, telling her to continue to glean his field. Boaz the man of God did not use his position to take advantage of her or the situation. Eventually, he met Ruth and had a conversation with her.

Here's the part that I feel qualified Boaz to be "the man." Naomi gave Ruth some inside information on how to let Boaz know she was interested in him, and Ruth did exactly as Naomi advised her to do. Boaz was cautious and was careful not to take advantage of Ruth.

> Then go and uncover his feet and lie down. He will tell you what to do."
> "I will do whatever you say," Ruth answered. So she went down to the threshing floor and did everything her mother-in-law told her to do.

> When Boaz had finished eating and drinking and was in good spirits, he went over to lie down at the far end of the grain pile. Ruth approached quietly, uncovered his feet and lay down. In the middle of the night something startled the man; he turned—and there was a woman lying at his feet!

> "Who are you?" he asked.

> "I am your servant Ruth," she said.

"Spread the corner of your garment over me, since you are a guardian-redeemer of our family."

"The Lord bless you, my daughter," he replied. "This kindness is greater than that which you showed earlier: You have not run after the younger men, whether rich or poor. And now, my daughter, don't be afraid. I will do for you all you ask. All the people of my town know that you are a woman of noble character. Although it is true that I am a guardian-redeemer of our family, there is another who is more closely related than I. Stay here for the night, and in the morning if he wants to do his duty as your guardian-redeemer, good; let him redeem you. But if he is not willing, as surely as the Lord lives I will do it. Lie here until morning."

So she lay at his feet until morning, but got up before anyone could be recognized; and he said, "No one must know that a woman came to the threshing floor." He also said, "Bring me the shawl you are wearing and hold it out." When she did so, he poured into it six measures of barley and placed the bundle on her. Then he went back to town (Ruth 3:4-15).

Now there are things in this story that sound quite strange when we try to interpret them according to modern cultural norms. But the thing that was the same then as it is now is that Boaz could have tried to take advantage of Ruth. However, he remained a man of God even in this potentially compromising position. How many of us would have given a woman like Ruth something for nothing? Boaz didn't provide for her just once, he did so again and again. Boaz protected her and her name. That is being a man of God.

Boaz was the man of God as the owner of the field. He was the man of God as the kinsmen redeemer, and he was being the man of God as a provider. What a great example Boaz is of what a man of God looks and acts like. No wonder they were both included in the lineage of Jesus Christ. How powerful is that?

Here's what I conclude from that story. When we are the men of God in all we do, we're also grafted into the family tree or lineage of Jesus Christ. Everything falls in line, and everything comes together when we are obedient to follow and do what the Lord calls us to do. It's not just that we are in the right company, but we are in the right place in all the situations of our lives.

4. Nehemiah

Let's discuss one more man who is worthy of the title man of God for his service and integrity. His name was Nehemiah and he also was the man of God in all the situations he had to face. We read,

> Also, our enemies said, "Before they know it or see us, we will be right there among them and will kill them and put an end to the work." Then the Jews

who lived near them came and told us ten times over, "Wherever you turn, they will attack us." Therefore I stationed some of the people behind the lowest points of the wall at the exposed places, posting them by families, with their swords, spears and bows.

After I looked things over, I stood up and said to the nobles, the officials and the rest of the people, "Don't be afraid of them. Remember the Lord, who is great and awesome, and fight for your families, your sons and your daughters, your wives and your homes."

When our enemies heard that we were aware of their plot and that God had frustrated it, we all returned to the wall, each to our own work. From that day on, half of my men did the work, while the other half were equipped with spears, shields, bows and armor. The officers posted themselves behind all the people of Judah who were building the wall. Those who carried materials did their work with one hand and held a weapon in the other, and each of the builders wore his sword at his side as he worked.

But the man who sounded the trumpet stayed with me. Then I said to the nobles, the officials and the rest of the people, "The work is extensive and spread out, and we are widely separated from each other along the wall. Wherever you hear the sound of the trumpet, join us there. Our God will fight for us!" (Nehemiah 4:11-20).

Nehemiah was involved in many stressful situations to say the least. Let's examine them for a moment. The nation of Israel was coming back from their exile to the Promised Land, where they were to face many problems. The people who were there did not want them to rebuild the walls and the Temple. Even though Nehemiah had permission from the Persian King Darius, the people of the land still plotted to kill all the Israelites who were trying to rebuild the city wall. The good news is that God frustrated their plans ... but God!

Nehemiah had to stay focused on the job at hand while at the same time encouraging the people to continue to work. This man of God trusted God in every situation. He was the man of God as the governor of the province. He was the man of God as the leader of the people. He was the man of God in the face of complete devastation and discouragement.

That is all so vital in my mind because many of us in the face of trials and tribulations fall apart and forget that God is even present. However, that wasn't the case with Nehemiah, for he trusted God even more when things looked bleak. He told the nobles and the leaders not to worry about their opponents because God was their shield. He reminded them that God was fighting for them.

The next time you find yourself in a struggle, I encourage you to stand fast on the truth and let the Lord be your strength. He is fighting for you and He is your shield.

Nehemiah was the man of God in all the situations in his life. So, as we can see there are men in the Bible who we can look at and say, "Here is a true man of God." The men we just looked at where not super men. They were just like us in every way. They had their problems and doubts, but when it came down to it, they trusted in the Lord when all the chips were down. You'll find yourself in trouble and in danger, maybe even facing temptation, but you must learn to trust in Jesus in those times.

Boaz and Nehemiah didn't have what we have, which is the Son of God on our side. They didn't have the added helper in the Holy Spirit who is with us, residing in us. It 's a can't-lose scenario for us if we stay true to who we are as men of God. The deck has been stacked in our favor and all we have to do is surrender and follow. We then become the men of God we are meant to be and our purpose and calling are set before us.

Listen to me, my brother. If Jesus doesn't change us, there's no way we can be saved — from sin or from ourselves. But like I said earlier, a life not changed is a life not surrendered. A life not surrendered is a life not saved. Jesus has to be our everything in order for all of this to work. I know those words may seem harsh and restrictive, but if we really want to be who we are called to be, and if we want to follow and honor Jesus, then we must surrender our lives and ourselves to Him. There can be no partial surrender in this. We can't have one foot in and one foot out of God's kingdom. It really is an all-or-nothing proposition.

My concern is that there are many of our brothers out there who are not fully surrendered to Jesus. In the end, this will be an issue. Jesus himself said that in the end, there will be those who say, "Lord, Lord did I not prophesy in your name? Did I not cast demons out in your name? and He will say, 'Be gone from me I never knew you.'" This means that these people will think they are saved, but they're not because they have never fully surrendered and then decided to follow Jesus. Therefore, they never had a true relationship with Him.

What they did was to make themselves believe what they wanted to believe. They believed a lie because there is no such thing as a partial follower of Jesus. It's all of Jesus or none of Jesus. In the same manner, it's all of you that's needed in order to be the man of God in all situations.

In conclusion, the answer to how you can be the man of God you're called to be in all your life roles is to trust in Jesus. He's the way, the truth, and the life. The problem we men have is that we are used to doing everything on our own. We think we have a bigger role to play in our transformation into the men of God we are called to be than we actually do. We try to make it happen on our own. We buy self-help books and try to be men and stand on our own two feet.

But remember, there are only three things we need to do. The first is to surrender to Jesus, allowing Him to change us. The second is to follow Jesus and the third is to be obedient to

His commands. As you can see, it starts with Jesus and ends with Him. Our ability to love the Lord our God with all our heart, mind, soul, and strength, and then to love our neighbors as we love ourselves all depends on Jesus.

Out of all the mighty men we have researched and spoken about, there's only one who was perfect – the perfect one Jesus Christ. He did it all totally right. He didn't sin and was the one man of God in every role He played. What's so great about Jesus is that the role He takes most seriously was being the Son of God. That role in His life took precedence over every other role, and every other role is the result of Him being a Son.

Isn't it ironic that the one who said it is the one who can make it happen in our lives? Jesus is also the one who transforms us into the men of God we are called to be. We just have to allow the transformation to infiltrate all our roles as men. My brother, let's let all of creation see the sons of God revealed. It starts with you.

God bless you!

FINAL THOUGHT

Here is my closing prayer for you.

Lord, I pray as my brothers read this book, they will choose to follow You, Jesus. That in return You change their lives as You have changed mine. That You, Jesus, make them into the one man of God in all they do as You are making me. I pray that all Your sons will love You with all their hearts, minds, and souls.

I also pray that as You make them like You, Jesus, that they will love like You love, Jesus, fulfilling the second great command. You are an awesome God and Father. You have shown us the way by giving us Your Son. Make us like Him, and let the creation see that the sons of God are revealed. In Jesus' name, I pray. Amen!

REFLECTION QUESTIONS

1. How do you compare to the men of God mentioned in this chapter?
2. Where is Jesus in your life?
3. Have you totally surrendered your life to Jesus?
4. Are you truly a man of God in all the roles you play?

ADDITIONAL REFERENCES

Ruth 3:4–15
Ruth 4:9–10
Nehemiah 4:11–20
Mark 15:21–22
Romans 16:13

The Eight Virtues of Rally Point Men's Ministries

At Rally Point Men's Ministries, we work to create the curriculum, tools, support, and fellowship necessary to continue building the integrity of God in men!

We have found that by implementing certain attitudes—or as we call them, virtues—causes a transformation to occur inside a man. Jesus' plan is to transform us from the inside out to form character in us as men and develop integrity from which we can then evangelize other men. Here are the eight Rally Point Men's Virtues we strive to teach and impart:

1. **Humility** is not thinking less of yourself but thinking of yourself less.

2. **Compassion** is thinking of others, understanding that you have fallen short so we are able to stand with those who fall short.

3. **Meekness** is control and discipline under pressure similar to how war horses allow themselves to be under the control of their rider, putting all their strength at their rider's disposal and direction.

4. **Passion** is directing your feelings to the right place and having a passionate love for God your Father.

5. **Mercy** is forgiving others because you have been forgiven.

6. **Purity** is keeping your heart and mind on the things of God as well as keeping your mind and thoughts pure before God.

7. **Diplomacy** is keeping the peace by being a peacemaker.

8. **Courage** is standing up for your faith and what you believe in. Courage does not mean absence of fear but acting correctly in the midst of fear.

MORE ABOUT
THE AUTHOR

WESLEY
PENNINGTON

Wesley Pennington grew up in Cranston, Rhode Island in a family of five boys and one girl, in which he is the youngest. He graduated from Cranston High School East and went on to study sociology at Western Connecticut State University. Wesley then became a member of the United States Army. He served a tour in Korea and upon coming back from Korea, he was assigned to the prestigious 82nd Airborne Division. During his time with the 82nd, Wesley was in one of the first groups sent to Operation Desert Storm.

Upon completion of his military commitment, he returned to Rhode Island where he worked for the West Warwick Police Department. After two-and-a-half years, he left there and went to work with the Rhode Island State Police where he has been employed since 1994. As coach of North Smithfield High School, Wesley's team won the 2019 State Championship and he received the 2019 Football Coach of the Year award. He currently serves as the football coach at West

Warwick High School. He is also an ordained pastor. Wesley is married to his wife, Marissa, and has two daughters, Ashley and Eliana.

You can find Wes's YouTube channel at

www.youtube.com/c/Wes'sManStuff

On Facebook

Facebook.com/RPmensministry

on Instagram

https://www.instagram.com/p/
CUuWhLsrQWu/

On LinkedIn

Linkedin.com/in/Wesley-pennington-
8575a13a/

contact him directly through his website

www.rallypointmensministries.org

or by email

wesley@rallypointconsultingllc.com

Made in the USA
Middletown, DE
09 August 2024

58726164R00076